HOW TO
ANALYZE PEOPLE
ON SIGHT

Each According To His Type

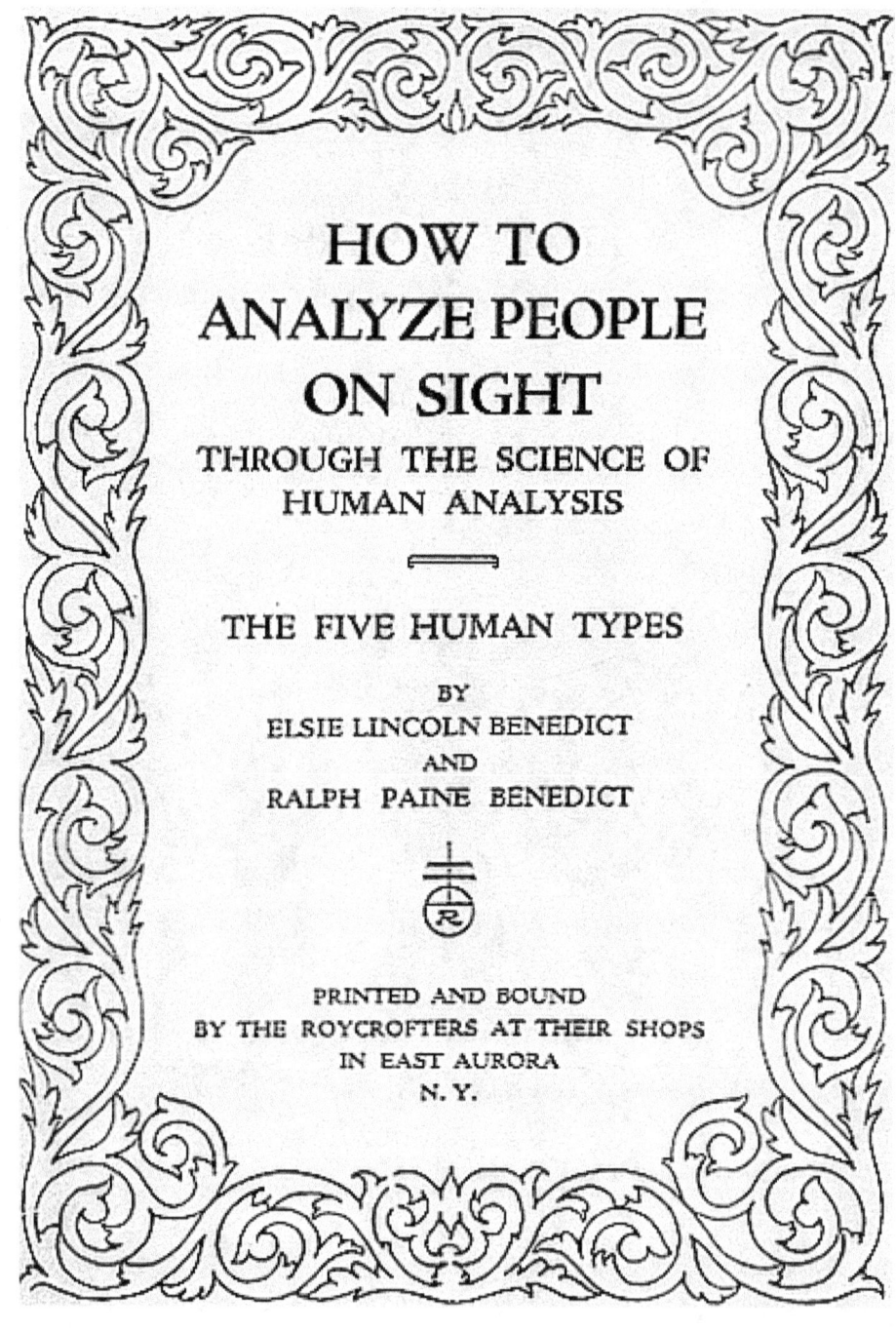

HOW TO ANALYZE PEOPLE ON SIGHT

THROUGH THE SCIENCE OF HUMAN ANALYSIS

THE FIVE HUMAN TYPES

BY
ELSIE LINCOLN BENEDICT
AND
RALPH PAINE BENEDICT

PRINTED AND BOUND
BY THE ROYCROFTERS AT THEIR SHOPS
IN EAST AURORA
N. Y.

Elsie Lincoln Benedict
and
Ralph Paine Benedict

WE THANK YOU

¶ To the following men and women we wish to express our appreciation for their share in the production of this book:

To Duren J. H. Ward, Ph. D.,
formerly of the Anthropology Department of Harvard University, who, as the discoverer of the fourth human type, has added immeasurably to the world's knowledge of human science.

To Raymond H. Lufkin,
of Boston, who made the illustrations for this volume scientifically accurate.

To The Roycrofters,
of East Aurora, whose artistic workmanship made it into a thing of beauty.

And last but not least,

To Sarah H. Young,
of San Francisco, our Business Manager, whose efficiency correlated all these and placed the finished product in the hands of our students.

THE AUTHORS

New York City,
June, 1921

DEDICATED
TO
OUR STUDENTS

What Leading Newspapers Say About Elsie Lincoln Benedict and Her Work

"Over fifty thousand people heard Elsie Lincoln Benedict at the City Auditorium during her six weeks lecture engagement in Milwaukee."—*Milwaukee Leader, April 2, 1921.*

"Elsie Lincoln Benedict has a brilliant record. She is like a fresh breath of Colorado ozone. Her ideas are as stimulating as the health-giving breezes of the Rockies."—*New York Evening Mail, April 16, 1914.*

"Several hundred people were turned away from the Masonic Temple last night where Elsie Lincoln Benedict, famous human analyst, spoke on 'How to Analyze People on Sight.' Asked how she could draw and hold a crowd of 3,000 for a lecture, she said: 'Because I talk on the one subject on earth in which every individual is most interested—himself.'"—*Seattle Times, June 2, 1920.*

"Elsie Lincoln Benedict is a woman who has studied deeply under genuine scientists and is demonstrating to thousands at the Auditorium each evening that she knows the connection between an individual's external characteristics and his inner traits."—*Minneapolis News, November 7, 1920.*

"Elsie Lincoln Benedict is known nationally, having conducted lecture courses in many of the large Eastern cities. Her work is based upon the practical methods of modern science as worked out in the world's leading laboratories where exhaustive tests are applied to determine individual types, talents, vocational bents and possibilities."—*San Francisco Bulletin, January 25, 1919.*

**It's not
how much you
know but what
you can
DO
that counts**

Human Analysis—The X-Ray

Modern science has proved that the fundamental traits of every individual are indelibly stamped in the shape of his body, head, face and hands—an X-ray by which you can read the characteristics of any person on sight.

The most essential thing in the world to any individual is to understand *himself*. The next is to understand the other fellow. For life is largely a problem of running your own car as it was built to be run, plus getting along with the other drivers on the highway.

From this book you are going to learn which type of car you are and the main reasons why you have not been getting the maximum of service out of yourself.

Also you are going to learn the makes of other human cars, and how to get the maximum of co-operation out of them. This co-operation is vital to happiness and success. We come in contact with our fellowman in all the activities of our lives and what we get out of life depends, to an astounding degree, on our relations with him.

Reaction to Environment

¶ The greatest problem facing any organism is successful reaction to its environment. Environment, speaking scientifically, is the sum total of your experiences. In plain United States, this means fitting vocationally, socially and maritally into the place where you are.

If you don't fit you must move or change your environment to fit *you*. If you can't change the environment and you won't move you will become a failure, just as tropical plants fail when transplanted to the Nevada desert.

Learn From the Sagebrush

¶ But there is something that grows and keeps on growing in the Nevada desert—the sagebrush. It couldn't move away and it couldn't change its waterless environment, so it did what you and I must do if we expect to succeed. It adapted itself to its environment, and there it stands, each little stalwart shrub a reminder of what even a plant can do when it tries!

Moving Won't Help Much

¶ Human life faces the same alternatives that confront all other forms of life—of adapting itself to the conditions under which it must live or becoming extinct. You have an advantage over the sagebrush in that you can move from your city or state or country to another, but after all that is not much of an advantage. For though you may improve your situation slightly you will still find that in any civilized country the main elements of your problem are the same.

Understand Yourself and Others

¶ So long as you live in a civilized or thickly populated community you will still need to understand your own nature and the natures of other people. No matter what you desire of life, other people's aims, ambitions and activities constitute vital obstructions along your pathway. You will never get far without the co-operation, confidence and comradeship of other men and women.

Primitive Problems

¶ It was not always so. And its recentness in human history may account for some of our blindness to this great fact.

In primitive times people saw each other rarely and had much less to do with each other. The human element was then not the chief problem. Their environmental problems had to do with such things as the elements, violent storms, extremes of heat and cold, darkness, the ever-present menace of wild beasts whose flesh was their food, yet who would eat them first unless they were quick in brain and body.

Civilization's Changes

¶ But all that is changed. Man has subjugated all other creatures and now walks the earth its supreme sovereign. He has discovered and invented and builded until now we live in skyscrapers, talk around the world without wires and by pressing a button turn darkness into daylight.

Causes of Failure

¶ Yet with all our knowledge of the outside world ninety-nine lives out of every hundred are comparative failures.

¶ The reason is plain to every scientific investigator. We have failed to study ourselves in relation to the great environmental problem of today. The stage-setting has been changed but not the play. The game is the same old game—you must adjust and adapt yourself to your environment or it will destroy you.

Mastering His Own Environment

¶ The cities of today *look* different from the jungles of our ancestors and we imagine that because the brain of man overcame the old menaces no new ones have arisen to take their place. We no longer fear extermination from cold. We turn on the heat. We are not afraid of the vast oceans which held our primitive forebears in thrall, but pass swiftly, safely and luxuriously over their surfaces. And soon we shall be breakfasting in New York and dining the same evening in San Francisco!

Facing New Enemies

¶ But in building up this stupendous superstructure of modern civilization man has brought into being a society so intricate and complex that he now faces the new environmental problem of human relationships.

The Modern Spider's Web

¶ Today we depend for life's necessities almost wholly upon the activities of others. The work of thousands of human hands and thousands of human brains lies back of every meal you eat, every journey you take, every book you read, every bed in which you sleep, every telephone conversation, every telegram you receive, every garment you wear.

And this fellowman of ours has multiplied, since that dim distant dawn, into almost two billion human beings, with at least one billion of them after the very things you want, and not a tenth enough to go around!

Adapt or Die

¶ Who will win? Nature answers for you. She has said with awful and inexorable finality that, whether you are a blade of grass on the Nevada desert or a man in the streets of London, you can win only as you adapt yourself to your environment. Today our environmental problem consists largely of the other fellow. Only those who learn to adapt themselves to their fellows can win great or lasting rewards.

Externals Indicate Internal Nature

¶ To do this it is necessary to better understand our neighbors—to recognize that people differ from each other in their likes and dislikes, traits, talents, tendencies and capabilities. The combination of these makes each individual's nature. It is not difficult to understand others for with each group of these traits there always goes its corresponding physical makeup—the externals whereby the internal is invariably indicated. This is true of every species on the globe and of every subdivision within each species.

Significance of Size, Shape and Structure

¶ All dogs belong to the same species but there is a great difference between the "nature" of a St. Bernard and that of a terrier, just as there is a decided difference between the natures of different human beings. But in both instances the actions, reactions and habits of each can be accurately anticipated on sight by the shape, size and structure of the two creatures.

Differences in Breed

¶ When a terrier comes into the room you instinctively draw away unless you want to be jumped at and greeted effusively. But you make no such movement to protect yourself from a St. Bernard because you read, on sight, the different natures of these two from their external appearance.

¶ You know a rose, a violet, a sunflower and an orchid and what perfume you are sure to find in each, by the same method. All are flowers and all belong to the same species, just as all human beings belong to the same species. But their respective size, shape and structure tell you in advance and on sight what their respective characteristics are.

The same is true of all human beings. They differ in certain fundamentals but always and invariably in accordance with their differences in size, shape and structure.

The Instinct of Self-Preservation

¶ The reason for this is plain. Goaded by the instinct of self-preservation, man, like all other living things, has made heroic efforts to meet the demands of his environment. He has been more successful than any other creature and is, as a result, the most complex organism on the earth. But his most baffling complexities resolve themselves into comparatively simple terms once it is recognized that each internal change brought about by his environment brought with it the corresponding external mechanism without which he could not have survived.

Interrelation of Body and Brain

¶ So today we see man a highly evolved creature who not only acts but thinks and feels. All these thoughts, feelings and emotions are interrelated.

The body and the mind of man are so closely bound together that whatever affects one affects the other. An instantaneous change of mind instantly changes the muscles of the face. A violent thought instantly brings violent bodily movements.

Movies and Face Muscles

¶ The moving picture industry—said to be the third largest in the world—is based largely on this interrelation. This industry would become extinct if something were to happen to sever the connection between external expressions and the internal nature of men and women.

Tells Fundamentals

¶ How much do external characteristics tell about a man? They tell, with amazing accuracy, all the basic, fundamental principal traits of his nature. The size, shape and structure of a man's body tell more important facts about his real self—what he thinks and what he does—than the average mother ever knows about her own child.

Learning to Read

¶ If this sounds impossible, if the seeming incongruity, multiplicity and heterogeneity of human qualities have baffled you, remember that this is exactly how the print in all books and newspapers baffled you before you learned to read.

Not long ago I was reading stories aloud to a three-year old. She wanted to "see the pictures," and when told there were none had to be shown the book.

"What funny little marks!" she cried, pointing to the print. "How do you get stories out of them?"

Printing looked to all of us at first just masses of meaningless little marks.

But after a few days at school how things did begin to clear up! It wasn't a jumble after all. There was something to it. It straightened itself out until the funny little marks became significant. Each of them had a meaning and the same meaning under all conditions. Through them your whole outlook on life became deepened and broadened—all because you learned the meaning of twenty-six little letters and their combinations!

Reading People

¶ Learning to read men and women is a more delightful process than learning to read books, for every person you see is a true story, more romantic and absorbing than any ever bound in covers.

Learning to read people is also a simpler process than learning to read books because there are fewer letters in the human alphabet. Though man seems to the untrained eye a mystifying mass of "funny little marks," he is not now difficult to analyze.

Only a Few Feelings

¶ This is because there are after all but a few kinds of human feelings. Some form of hunger, love, hate, fear, hope or ambition gives rise to every human emotion and every human thought.

Thoughts Bring Actions

¶ Now our actions follow our thoughts. Every thought, however transitory, causes muscular action, which leaves its trace in that part of the physical organism which is most closely allied to it.

Physiology and Psychology Interwoven

¶ Look into the mirror the next time you are angry, happy, surprised, tired or sorrowful and note the changes wrought by your emotions in your facial muscles.

Constant repetition of the same kinds of thoughts or emotions finally makes permanent changes in that part of the body which is physiologically related to these mental processes.

The Evolution of the Jaw

¶ The jaw is a good illustration of this alliance between the mind and the body. Its muscles and bones are so closely allied to the pugnacity instinct center in the brain that the slightest thought of combat causes the jaw muscles to stiffen. Let the thought of any actual physical encounter go through your mind and your jaw bone will automatically move upward and outward.

After a lifetime of combat, whether by fists or words, the jaw sets permanently a little more upward and outward—a little more like that of the bulldog. It keeps to this combative mold, "because," says Mother Nature, the great efficiency expert, "if you are going to call on me constantly to stiffen that jaw I'll fix it so it will stay that way and save myself the trouble."

Inheritance of Acquired Traits

¶ Thus the more combative jaw, having become permanent in the man's organism, can be passed on to his children.

¶ Right here comes a most interesting law and one that has made possible the science of Human Analysis:

Law of Size

¶ *The larger any part or organ the better its equipment for carrying out the work of that organ and the more does it tend to express itself.* Nature IS an efficiency expert and doesn't give you an oversupply of anything without demanding that you use it.

Jaws Becoming Smaller

¶ Our ancestors developed massive jaws as a result of constant combat. As fast as civilization decreased the necessity for combat Nature decreased the size of the average human jaw.

Meaning of the Big Jaw

¶ But wherever you see a large protruding jaw you see an individual "armed and engined," as Kipling says, for some kind of fighting. The large jaw always goes with a combative nature, whether it is found on a man or a woman, a child, a pugilist or a minister.

Exhibit A—The Irishman

¶ The large jaw, therefore, is seen to be both a result and a cause of certain things. As the inheritance of a fighting ancestor it is the result of millions of years of fighting in prehistoric times, and, like any other over-developed part or organ, it has an intense urge to express itself. This inherent urge is what makes the owner of that jaw "fight at the drop of the hat," and often have "a chip on his shoulder."

Natural Selection

¶ Thus, because every external characteristic is the result of natural laws, and chiefly of natural selection, the vital traits of any creature can be read from his externals. Every student of biology, anatomy, anthropology, ethnology or psychology is familiar with these facts.

Built to Fit

¶ Man's organism has developed, altered, improved and evolved "down through the slow revolving years" with one instinctive aim—successful reaction to its environment. Every part has been laboriously constructed to that sole end. Because of this its functions are marked as clearly upon it as those of a grain elevator, a steamship or a piano.

Survival of the Fittest

¶ Nature has no accidents, she wastes no material and everything has a purpose. If you put up a good fight to live she will usually come to your rescue and give you enough of whatever is needed to tide you over. If you don't, she says you are not fit to people the earth and lets you go without a pang. Thus she weeds out all but the strong—and evolution marches on.

Causes of Racial Characteristics

¶ This inherent potentiality for altering the organism to meet the demands of the environment is especially noticeable in races and is the reason for most racial differences.

Differences in environment—climate, altitude and topography necessitated most of these physical differentiations which today enable us to know at a glance whether a man belongs to the white race, the yellow race, or the black race. The results of these differentiations and modifications will be told in the various chapters of this book.

Types Earlier than Races

¶ The student of Human Analysis reads the disposition and nature of every individual with ease regardless of whether that individual be an American, a Frenchman, a Kaffir or a Chinaman, because Human Analysis explains those fundamental traits which run through every race, color and nationality, according to the externals which always go with those traits.

Five Biological Types

¶ *Human Analysis differs from every other system of character analysis in that it classifies man, for the first time, into five types according to his biological evolution.*

¶ It deals with man in the light of the most recent scientific discoveries. It estimates each individual according to his "human" qualities rather than his "character" or so-called "moral" qualities. In other words, it takes his measure as a human being and determines from his externals his chances for success in the world of today.

These Rules Work

¶ Every rule in this book is based on scientific data, has been proved to be accurate by investigations and surveys of all kinds of people in all parts of the world.

These rules do not work merely *part* of the time. They work *all* the time, under all conditions and apply to every individual of every race, every color, every country, every community and every family.

Through this latest human science you can learn to read people as easily as you read books—if you will take the little time and pains to learn the rules which compose your working alphabet.

Do What We Want to Do

¶ It is easy to know what an individual will do under most circumstances because every human being does what he *wants* to do in the *way* he prefers to do it *most* of the time. If you doubt it try this test: bring to mind any intimate friends, or even that husband or wife, and note how few changes they have made in their way of doing things in twenty years!

Preferences Inborn

¶ Every human being is born with preferences and predilections which manifest themselves from earliest childhood to death. These inborn tendencies are never obliterated and seldom controlled to any great extent, and then only by individuals who have learned the power of the mind over the body. Inasmuch as this knowledge is possessed by only a few, most of the people of the earth are blindly following the dictates of their inborn leanings.

Follow Our Bents

¶ In other words, more than ninety-nine per cent of all the people you know are following their natural bents in reacting to all their experiences—from the most trivial incidents to the most far-reaching emergencies.

"Took It" From Grandmother

¶ The individual is seldom conscious of these habitual acts of his, much less of where he got them. The nearest he comes is to say he "got it from his father" or "she takes it from grandmother." But where did grandmother get it?

Man No Mystery

¶ Science has taken the trouble to investigate and today we know not only where grandmother got it but what she did with it. She got it along with her size, shape and structure—in other words, from her type—and she did just what you and everybody else does with his type-characteristics. She acted in accordance with her type just as a canary sings like a canary instead of talking like a parrot, and just as a rose gives off rose perfume instead of violet.

This law holds throughout every species and explains man—who likes to think himself a deep mystery—as it explains every other creature.

The Hold of Habit

¶ Look around you in shop, office, field or home and you will find that the quick, alert, impulsive man is acting quickly, alertly and impulsively most of the time. Nothing less than a calamity slows him down and then only temporarily; while the slow, patient, mild and passive individual is acting slowly, patiently, mildly and passively in spite of all goads. Some overwhelming passion or crisis may speed him up momentarily but as soon as it fades he reverts to his old slow habits.

Significance of Fat, Bone and Muscle

¶ Human Analysis is the new science which shows you how to recognize the slow man, the quick man, the stubborn man, the yielding man, the leader, the learner, and all other basic kinds of men on sight from the shape, size and structure of their bodies.

Certain bodily shapes indicate predispositions to fatness, leanness, boniness, muscularity and nervousness, and this predisposition is so much a part of the warp and woof of the individual that he can not disguise it. The urge given him by this inborn mechanism is so strong as to be practically irresistible. Every experience of his life calls forth some kind of reaction and invariably the reaction will be similar, in every vital respect, to the reactions of other people who have bodies of the same general size, shape and structure as his own.

Succeed at What We Like

¶ No person achieves success or happiness when compelled to do what he naturally dislikes to do. Since these likes and dislikes stay with him to the grave, one of the biggest modern problems is that of helping men and women to discover and to capitalize their inborn traits.

Enthusiasm and Self-Expression

¶ Every individual does best those things which permit him to act in accordance with his natural bents. This explains why we like best those things we do best. It takes real enthusiasm to make a success of any undertaking for nothing less than enthusiasm can turn on a full current.

We struggle from the cradle to the grave for self-expression and everything that pushes us in a direction opposed to our natural tendencies is done half-heartedly, inefficiently and disgruntledly. These are the steps that lead straight to failure. Yet failure can be avoided and success approximated by every normal person if he will take the same precaution with his own machinery that he takes with his automobile.

Learn to Drive Your Car

¶ If you were presented with a car by your ancestors—which is precisely what happened to you at birth—you would not let an hour go by without finding out what make or type of car it was. Before a week elapsed you would have taken the time, labor and interest to learn how to run it,—not merely any old way, but the *best* way for that particular make of car.

Five Makes of Human Cars

¶ There are five makes or types of human cars, differing as definitely in size, shape and structure as Fords differ from Pierce-Arrows. Each human type differs as widely in its capacities, possibilities and aptitudes as a Ford differs from a Pierce-Arrow. Like the Ford or Pierce the externals indicate these

14

functional differences with unfailing accuracy. Furthermore just as a Ford never changes into a Pierce nor a Pierce into a Ford, a human being never changes his type. He may modify it, train it, polish it or control it somewhat, but he will never change it.

Can Not be Deceived

¶ The student of Human Analysis cannot be deceived as to the type of any individual any more than you can be deceived about the make of a car.

One may "doll up" a Ford to his heart's content—remove the hood and top and put on custom-made substitutes—it is still a Ford, always will be a Ford and you can always detect that it is a Ford. It will do valuable, necessary things but only those things it was designed to do and in its own particular manner; nor could a Pierce act like a Ford.

Are You a Ford or a Pierce?

¶ So it is with human cars. Maybe you have been awed by the jewels and clothes with which many human Fords disguise themselves. The chances are that you have overlooked a dozen Pierces this week because their paint was rusty. Perchance you are a Pierce yourself, drawing a Ford salary because you don't know you are a high-powered machine capable of making ten times the speed you have been making on your highway of life.

Superficialities Sway Us

¶ If so your mistake is only natural. The world classifies human beings according to their superficialities. To the world a human motorcycle can pass for a Rolls-Royce any day if sufficiently camouflaged with diamonds, curls, French heels and plucked eyebrows.

Bicycles in Congress

¶ In the same manner many a bicycle in human form gets elected to Congress because he plays his machinery for all it is worth and gets a hundred per cent service out of it. Every such person learned early in life what kind of car he was and capitalized its natural tendencies.

Don't Judge by Veneer

¶ Nothing is more unsafe than to attempt to judge the actual natures of people by their clothes, houses, religious faith, political affiliations, prejudices, dialect, etiquette or customs. These are only the veneer laid on by upbringing, teachers, preachers, traditions and other forces of suggestion, and it is a veneer so thin that trifles scratch it off.

The Real Always There

¶ But the real individual is always there, filled with the tendencies of his type, bending always toward them, constantly seeking opportunities to run as he was built to run, forever striving toward self-expression. It is this ever-active urge which causes him to revert, in the manifold activities of everyday life, to the methods, manners and peculiarities common to his type.

This means that unless he gets into an environment, a vocation and a marriage which permits of his doing what he *wants* to do he will be miserable, inefficient, unsuccessful and sometimes criminal.

Causes of Crime

¶ That this is the true explanation of crime has been recognized for many years by leading thinkers. Two prison wardens—Thomas Tynan of Colorado and Thomas Mott Osborne of Sing Sing—effectively initiated penal reforms based upon it.

Every crime, like every personal problem, arises from some kind of situation wherein instinct is thwarted by outside influence.

¶ Human Analysis teaches you to recognize, on sight, the predominant instincts of any individual—in brief, what that individual is inclined to do under all the general situations of his life. You know what the world tries to compel him to do. If the discrepancy between these two is beyond the reach of his type he refuses to do what society demands. This and this only is back of every human digression from indiscretion to murder.

It is as vain to expect to eradicate these inborn trends and put others in their places as to make a sewing machine out of an airplane or an oak out of a pine. The most man can do for his neighbor is to understand and inspire him. The most he can do for himself is to understand and organize his inborn capacities.

Find Your Own Type

¶ The first problem of your happiness is to find out what type you are yourself—which you will know after reading this book—and to build your future accordingly.

Knowing and Helping Others

¶ The second is to learn how to analyze others to the end that your relationships with them may be harmonious and mutually advantageous.

Take every individual according to the way he was born, accept him as that kind of mechanism and deal with him in the manner befitting that mechanism. In this way and this only will you be able to impress or to help others.

In this way only will you be able to achieve real success. In this way only will you be able to help your fellowman find the work, the environment and the marriage wherein he can be happy and successful.

The Four C's

¶ To get the maximum of pleasure and knowledge out of this interesting course there are four things to remember as *your* part of the contract.

Read CONCENTRATEDLY

¶ Think of *what* you are reading *while* you are reading it. Concentration is a very simple thing. The next C is

Observe CAREFULLY

¶ Look at people carefully (but not starefully) when analyzing them. Don't jump at conclusions. We humans have a great way of twisting facts to fit our conclusion as soon as we have made one. But don't spend all your time getting ready to decide and forget to decide at all, like the man who was going to jump a ditch. He ran so far back to get a good start each time that he never had the strength to jump when he got there. Get a good start by observing carefully. Then

Decide CONFIDENTLY

¶ Be sure you are right and then go ahead. Make a decision and make it with the confidence that you are right. If you will determine now to follow this rule it will compel you to follow the first two because, in order to be sure you are right, to be certain you are not misjudging anybody, you will read each rule concentratedly and observe each person carefully beforehand.

Practise CONSTANTLY

¶ "Practice makes perfect." Take this for your motto if you would become expert in analyzing people. It is one easily followed for you come in contact with people everywhere—at home, amongst your business associates, with your friends and on the street. Remember you can only benefit from a thing as you use it. A car that you never took out of the garage would be of no value to you. So get full value out of this course by using it at all times.

These Rules Your Tools

¶ These rules are scientific. They are true and they are true always. They are very valuable tools for the furtherance of your progress through life.

An understanding of people is the greatest weapon you can possess. Therefore these are the most precious tools you can own. But like every tool in the world and all knowledge in the world, they must be used as they were built to be used or you will get little service out of them.

You would not expect to run a car properly without paying the closest attention to the rules for clutches, brakes, starters and gears. Everything scientific is based not on guesses but laws. This course in Analyzing People on Sight is as scientific as the automobile. It will carry you far and do it easily if you will do your part. Your part consists of learning the few simple rules laid down in this book and in applying them in the everyday affairs of your life.

Fewer and Truer

¶ Many things which have been found to be true in almost every instance could have been included in this course. But we prefer to make fewer statements and have those of bedrock certainty. Therefore this course, like all our courses, consists exclusively of those facts which have been found to be true in every particular of people in normal health.

IMPORTANT

The Five Extremes

¶ This book deals with PURE or UNMIXED types only. When you understand these, the significance of their several combinations as seen in everyday life will be clear to you.

The Human Alphabet

¶ Just as you can not understand the meaning of a word until you know the letters that go into the makeup of that word, you cannot analyze people accurately until you get these five extreme types firmly in your mind, for they are your alphabet.

Founded in Five Biological Systems

¶ Each PURE type is the result of the over-development of one of the five biological systems possessed by all human beings—the nutritive, circulatory, muscular, bony or nervous.

Therefore every individual exhibits to some degree the characteristics of all the five types.

The Secret of Individuality

¶ But his PREDOMINANT traits and INDIVIDUALITY—the things that make him the KIND of man he is—agree infallibly with whichever one of the five systems PREDOMINATES in him.

Combinations Common in America

¶ The average American man or woman is a COMBINATION of some two of these types with a third discernible in the background.

To Analyze People

¶ To understand human beings familiarize yourself first with the PURE or UNMIXED types and then it will be easy and fascinating to spell out their combinations and what they mean in the people all about you.

Postpone Combinations

¶ Until you have learned these pure types thoroughly it will be to your advantage to forget that there is such a thing as combinations. After you have these extreme types well in mind you will be ready to analyze combinations.

The Five Types

¶ Science has discovered that there are five types of human beings. Discarding for a moment their technical names, they may be called the fat people, the florid people, the muscular people, the bony people and the mental people.

Each varies from the others in shape, size and structure and is recognizable at a glance by his physique or build. This is because his type is determined by the preponderance within his body of one of the five great departments or biological systems—the nutritive, the circulatory, the muscular, the bony or the nervous.

At Birth

¶ Every child is born with one of these systems more highly developed, larger and better equipped than the others.

Type Never Disappears

¶ Throughout his life this system will express itself more, be more intense and constant in its functioning than the others and no manner of training, education, environment or experience, so long as he remains in normal health, will alter the predominance of this system nor prevent its dictating his likes, dislikes and most of his reactions.

Effect of Eating

¶ If you do not understand why the overaction of one bodily system should influence a man's nature see if you can't recall more than one occasion when a square meal made a decided difference in your disposition within the space of thirty minutes.

If one good meal has the power to alter so completely our personalities temporarily, is it then any wonder that constant overfeeding causes everybody to love a fat man? For the fat man is habitually and chronically in that beatific state which comes from over-eating.

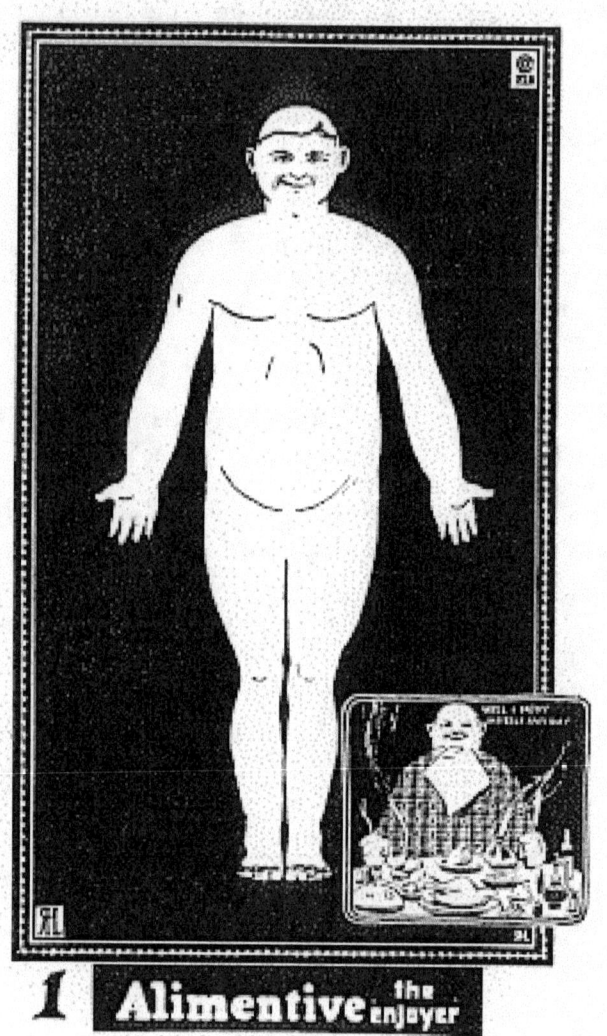

1 **Alimentive** the enjoyer

CHAPTER I

The Alimentive Type

"The Enjoyer"

Note: Bear in mind at the beginning of this and every other chapter, that we are describing the extreme or unmixed type. Before leaving this book you will understand combination types and should read people as readily as you now read your newspaper.

hose individuals in whom the alimentive system is more highly developed than any other are called Alimentives. The alimentive system consists of the stomach, intestines, alimentary canal and every part of the assimilative apparatus.

Physical Rotundity

¶ A general rotundity of outline characterizes this type. He is round in every direction. Fat rolls away from his elbows, wrists, knees and shoulders. (See Chart 1)

The Fat, Overweight Individual

¶ Soft flesh thickly padded over a small-boned body distinguishes the pure Alimentive type. In men of this type the largest part of the body is around the girth; in women it is around the hips. These always indicate a large nutritive system in good working order. Fat is only surplus tissue—the amount manufactured by the assimilative system over and above the needs of the body.

Fat is more soft and spongy than bone or muscle and lends to its wearer a softer structure and appearance.

Small Hands and Feet

¶ Because his bones are small the pure Alimentive has small feet and small hands. How many times you have noted with surprise that the two hundred pound woman had tiny feet! The inconvenience of "getting around" which you have noticed in her is due to the fact that while she has more weight to carry she has smaller than average feet with which to do it.

The Pure Alimentive Head

¶ A head comparatively small for the body is another characteristic of the extreme Alimentive. The neck and lower part of the head are covered with rolls of fat. This gives the head the effect of spreading outward from the crown as it goes down to the neck, thus giving the neck a short, disproportionately large appearance.

The Round-Faced Person

¶ A "full-moon" face with double or triple chins gives this man his "baby face." (See Chart 2) Look carefully at any extremely fat person and you will see that his features are inclined to the same immaturity of form that characterizes his body.

Very few fat men have long noses. Nearly all fat men and women have not only shorter, rounder noses but shorter upper lips, fuller mouths, rounder eyes and more youthful expressions than other people—in short, the features of childhood.

The entire physical makeup of this type is modeled upon the circle—round hands with dimples where the knuckles are supposed to be; round fingers, round feet, round waist, round limbs, sloping shoulders, curving thighs, bulging calves, wrists and ankles.

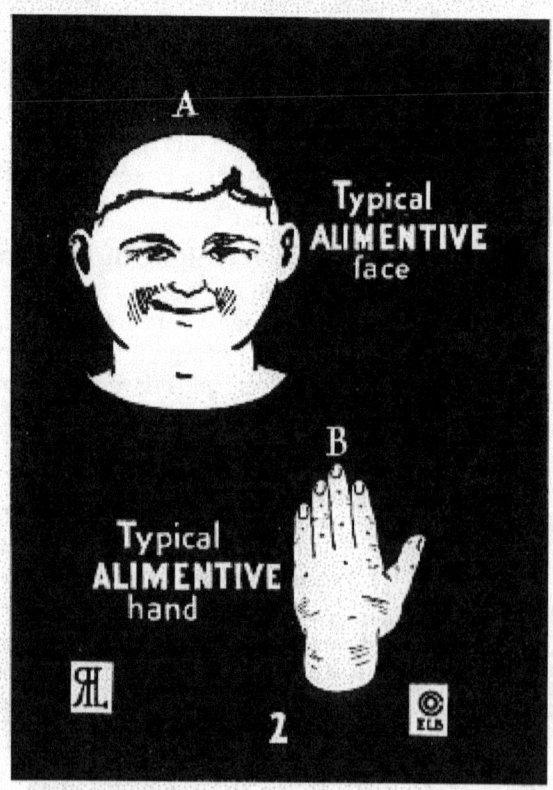

A
Typical
ALIMENTIVE
face

B

Typical
ALIMENTIVE
hand

2

Wherever you see curves predominating in the physical outlines of any person, that person is largely of the Alimentive type and will always exhibit alimentive traits.

The Man of Few Movements

¶ The Alimentive is a man of unhurried, undulating movements. The difficulty in moving large bodies quickly necessitates a slowing down of all his activities. These people are easeful in their actions, make as few moves as possible and thereby lend an air of restfulness wherever they go.

Because it is difficult to turn their heads, extremely fat people seldom are aware of what goes on behind them.

The Fat Man's Walk

¶ Very fat people waddle when they walk, though few of them realize it. They can not watch themselves go by and no one else has the heart to impart bad news to this pleasant person.

Spilling Over Chairs

¶ The fat man spills over chairs and out of his clothes. Big arm chairs, roomy divans and capacious automobiles are veritable dykes to these men. Note the bee-line the fat person makes for the big leather chair when he enters a room!

Clothes for Comfort

¶ The best that money can buy are the kinds of clothes purchased by the Alimentive whenever he can afford them. And it often happens that he can afford them, especially if the Cerebral system comes second in his makeup. If he is in middle circumstances his clothes will be chosen chiefly for comfort. Even the rich Alimentive "gets into something loose" as soon as he is alone. Baggy trousers, creased sleeves, soft collars and soft cuffs are seen most frequently on fat men.

Comfort is one of the very first aims of this type. To attain it he often wears old shoes or gloves long past their time to save breaking in a new pair.

Susceptible to Cold

¶ Cold weather affects this type. If you will look about you the first cold day of autumn you will note that most of the overcoats are on the plump men.

How the Fat Man Talks

¶ Never to take anything too seriously is an unconscious policy of fat people. They show it plainly in their actions and speech. The very fat man is seldom a brilliant conversationalist. He is often a "jollier" and tells stories well, especially anecdotes and personal experiences.

Doesn't Tell His Troubles

¶ He seldom relates his troubles and often appears not to have any. He avoids references to isms and ologies and gives a wide berth to all who deal in them. Radical groups seldom number any extremely fat men among their members, and when they do it is usually for some other purpose than those mentioned in the by-laws.

The very fat man dislikes argument, avoids disagreeing with you and sticks to the outer edges of serious questions in his social conversation.

The Fat Man "Lives to Eat"

¶ Rich food in large quantities is enjoyed by the average fat man three times a day and three hundred and sixty-five days a year. Between meals he usually manages to stow away a generous supply of candy, ice cream, popcorn and fruit. We have interviewed countless popcorn and fruit vendors on this subject and every one of them told us that the fat people kept them in business.

Visits the Soda Fountain Often

¶ As for the ice cream business, take a look the next time you pass a soda fountain and note the large percentage of fat people joyfully scooping up mountains of sundaes, parfaits and banana splits. You will find that of those who are sipping things through straws the thin folks are negotiating lemonades and phosphates, while a creamy frappé is rapidly disappearing from the fat man's glass.

The Deep Mystery

¶ "What do you suppose is making me so plump?" naively inquires the fat man when it finally occurs to him—as it did to his friends long before—that he is surely and speedily taking on flesh.

If you don't know the answer, look at the table of any fat person in any restaurant, café or dining room. He is eating with as much enthusiasm as if he had just been rescued from a forty-day fast, instead of having only a few hours before looked an equally generous meal in the eye and put it all under his belt. The next time you are at an American plan hotel where meals are restricted to certain hours note how the fat people are always the first ones into the dining room when the doors are opened!

Fat-Making Foods

¶ Butter, olive oil, cream, pastry and starches are foods that increase your weight just as fast as you eat them, if your assimilative system is anything like it should be. Though he is the last man in the world who ought to indulge in them the fat man likes these foods above all others and when compelled to have a meal without them feels as though he hadn't eaten at all.

Why They Don't Lose Weight

¶ We had a friend who decided to reduce. But in spite of the fact that she lived on salads almost exclusively for a week she kept right on gaining. We thought she had been surreptitiously treating herself to lunches between meals until some one noticed the dressing with which she drowned her lettuce: pure olive oil—a cupful at a sitting—"because," she said "I must have something tasty to camouflage the stuff."

An Experiment

¶ Once in California, where no city block is complete without its cafeteria, we took a committee from one of our Human Analysis classes to six of these big establishments one noontime. To illustrate to them the authenticity of the facts we have stated above we prophesied what the fat ones would select for their meals.

Without exception their trays came by heaped with pies, cake, cream, starchy vegetables and meat, just as we predicted.

A Short Life But a Merry One

¶ According to the statistics of the United States Life Insurance Companies fat people die younger than others. And the Insurance Companies ought to know, for upon knowing instead of guessing what it is that takes us off, depends the whole life insurance business. That they consider the extremely fat man an unsafe risk after thirty years of age is a well-known fact.

"I am interrupted every day by salesmen for everything on earth except one. But the life insurance agents leave me alone!" laughed a very fat young lawyer friend of ours the other morning—and he went on ordering ham and eggs, waffles, potatoes and coffee!

That he is eating years off his life doesn't trouble the fat man, however. He has such a good time doing it!

"I Should Worry," Says the Fat Man

¶ It was no accident that "Ish ka bibble" was invented by the Hebrew. For this race has proportionately more fat people in it than any other and fat people just naturally believe worry is useless. But the fat man gets this philosophy from the same source that gives him most of his other traits—his predominating system.

Digestion and Contentment

¶ The eating of delicious food is one of the most intense and poignant pleasures of life. The digestion of food, when one possesses the splendid machinery for it which characterizes the Alimentive, gives a deep feeling of serenity and contentment.

Since the fat man is always just going to a big meal or in the process of digesting one he does not give himself a chance to become ill natured. His own and the world's troubles sit lightly upon him.

The Most Popular Type Socially

¶ "The life of the party" is the fat man or that pleasing, adaptable, feminine creature, the fat woman. No matter what comes or goes they have a good time and it is such an infectious one that others catch it from them.

Did you ever notice how things pick up when the fat ones appear? Every hostess anticipates their arrival with pleasure and welcomes them with relief. She knows that she can relax now, and sure enough, Fatty hasn't his hat off till the atmosphere shows improvement. By the time Chubby gets into the parlor and passes a few of her sunny remarks the wheels are oiled for the evening and they don't run down till the last plump guest has said good night.

¶ So it is no wonder that fat people spend almost every evening at a party. They get so many more invitations than the rest of us!

Likes Complacent People

¶ People who take things as they find them are the ones the Alimentive prefers for friends, not only because, like the rest of us, he likes his own kind of folks, but because the other kind seem incongruous to him. He takes the attitude that resistance is a waste of energy. He knows other and easier ways of getting what he desires.

There are types who take a lively interest in those who are different from them, but not the Alimentive. He prefers easy-going, hospitable, complacent friends whose homes and hearts are always open and whose minds run on the simple, personal things.

¶ The reason for this is obvious. All of us like the people, situations, experiences and environments which bring out our natural tendencies, which call into play those reflexes and reactions to which we tend naturally.

Chooses Food-Loving Friends

¶ "Let's have something to eat" is a phrase whose hospitality has broken more ice and warmed more hearts than any other, unless perchance that rapidly disappearing "let's have something to drink." The fat person keeps at the head of his list those homey souls who set a good table and excel in the art of third and fourth helpings.

Because he is a very adaptable sort of individual this type can reconcile himself to the other kind whenever it serves his purpose. But the tenderest spots in his heart are reserved for those who encourage him in his favorite indoor sport.

When He Doesn't Like You

¶ A fat man seldom dislikes anybody very hard or for very long.

Really disliking anybody requires the expenditure of a good deal of energy and hating people is the most strenuous work in the world. So the Alimentive refuses to take even his dislikes to heart. He is a consistent conserver of steam and this fact is one of the secrets of his success.

He applies this principle to everything in life. So he travels smoothly through his dealings with others.

Holds Few Grudges

¶ "Forget it" is another phrase originated by the fat people. You will hear them say it more often than any other type. And what is more, they excel the rest of us in putting it into practice. The result is that their nerves are usually in better working order. This type runs down his batteries less frequently than any other.

Avoids the "Ologists"

¶ When he takes the trouble to think about it there are a few kinds of people the Alimentive does not care for. The man who is bent on discussing the problems of the universe, the highbrow who wants to practise his new relativity lecture on him, the theorist who is given to lengthy expatiations, and all advocates of new isms and ologies are avoided by the pure Alimentive. He calls them faddists, fanatics and fools.

When he sees a highbrow approaching, instead of having it out with him as some of the other types would, he finds he has important business somewhere else. Thus he preserves his temperature, something that in the average fat man seldom goes far above normal.

No Theorist

¶ Theories are the bane of this type. He just naturally doesn't believe in them. Scientific discoveries, unless they have to do with some new means of adding to his personal comforts, are taboo. The next time this one about "fat men dying young" is mentioned in his presence listen to his jolly roar. The speed with which he disposes of it will be beautiful to see!

"Say, I feel like a million dollars!" he will assure you if you read this chapter to him. "And I'll bet the folks who wrote that book are a pair of grouches who have forgotten what a square meal tastes like!"

Where the T-Bones Go

¶ When you catch a three-inch steak homeward bound you will usually find it tucked under the arm of a well-rounded householder. When his salary positively prohibits the comforts of parlor, bedroom and other parts of the house the fat man will still see to it that the kitchen does not lack for provender.

Describes His Food

¶ The fat person likes to regale you with alluring descriptions of what he had for breakfast, what he has ordered for lunch and what he is planning for dinner—and the rarebit he has on the program for after the theater.

Eats His Way to the Grave

¶ Most of us are committing suicide by inches in one form or another—and always in that form which is inherent in our type.

The Alimentive eats his way to the grave and has at least this much to say for it: it is more delightful than the pet weaknesses by which the other types hasten the final curtain.

Diseases He Is Most Susceptible To

¶ Diabetes is more common among this type than any other. Apoplexy comes next, especially if the fat man is also a florid man with a fast heart or an inclination to high blood pressure. A sudden breaking down of any or several of the vital organs is also likely to occur to fat people earlier than to others. It is the price they pay for their years of over-eating.

¶ Overtaxed heart, kidneys and liver are inevitable results of too much food.

So the man you call "fat and husky" is fat but *not* husky, according to the statistics.

Fat Men and Influenza

¶ During the historic Spanish Influenza epidemic of 1918 more fat people succumbed than all other types combined. This fact was a source of surprise and much discussion on the part of newspapers, but not of the scientists. The big question in treating this disease and its twin, Pneumonia, is: will the heart hold out? Fat seriously handicaps the heart.

The Fat Man's Ford Engine

¶ The human heart weighs less than a pound but it is the one organ in all our machinery that never takes a rest. It is the engine of the human car, and what a faithful little motor too—like the Ford engine which it so much resembles. If you live to be forty it chugs away forty years, and if you stay here ninety it stretches it to ninety, without an instant of vacation.

But it must be treated with consideration and the first consideration is not to overwork it. A Ford engine is large enough for a Ford car, for Fords are light weight. As long as you do not weigh too much your engine will carry you up the hills and down the dales of life with good old Ford efficiency and at a pretty good gait.

Making a Truck out of Your Ford

¶ But when you take on fat you are doing to your engine what a Ford driver would be doing to his if he loaded his car with brick or scrap iron.

A Ford owner who intended to transport bricks the rest of his life could get a big-cylinder engine and substitute it for the original but you can't do that. This little four-cylinder affair is the only one you will ever have and no amount of money, position or affection can buy you a new one if you mistreat it. Like the Ford engine, it will stand for a good many pounds of excess baggage and still do good work. But if you load on too much and keep it there the day will come when its cylinders begin to skip.

¶ You may take it to the service station and pay the doctors to grind the valves, fix your carbureter and put in some new spark plugs. These may work pretty well as long as you are traveling the paved highway of Perfect Health; you may keep up with the procession without noticing anything particularly wrong.

But come to the hill of Pneumonia or Diabetes and you are very likely not to make the grade.

Don't "Kill Your Engine"

¶ The records in America show that thousands of men and women literally "kill their engines" every year when they might have lived many years longer.

How Each Finds Happiness

¶ We live for happiness and each type finds its greatest happiness in following those innate urges determined by the most highly-developed system in its makeup.

The Alimentive's disposition, nature, character and personality are built by and around his alimentary system. He is happiest when gratifying it and whenever he thwarts it he is miserable, just as the rest of us are when we thwart our predominant system.

The World Needs Him

¶ This type has so many traits needed by the world, however, and has such extreme capacity for enjoying life that the race, not to mention himself, would profit greatly by his denying himself excessive amounts of food.

Enjoyment the Keynote of This Type

¶ The good things of life—rich, abundant food and everything that serves the personal appetites—are the cravings of this type.

He purchases and uses more of the limousines, yachts and chefs than any other three types combined, and gets more for his money out of them than others do. The keynote of his nature is personal enjoyment. His senses of touch and taste are also especially acute.

The Fat Man Loves Comfort

¶ You can tell a great deal about a man's type by noting for what classes of things he spends most of his extra money.

The Alimentive may have no fire insurance, no Liberty bonds, no real estate but he will have all the modern comforts he can possibly afford.

Most of the world's millionaires are fat and Human Analysis explains why. We make few efforts in life save to satisfy our most urgent demands, desires, and ambitions. Each human type differs in its cravings from each of the others and takes the respective means necessary to gratify these cravings.

The Alimentive craves those luxuries, comforts and conveniences which only money can procure for him.

The Fat Millionaire

¶ When the Alimentive is a man of brains he uses his brains to get money. No fat person enjoys work but the greater his brain capacity the more will he forego leisure to make money.

When the Fat Man is in Average Circumstances

¶ Any man's money-making ambitions depend largely on whether money is essential to the satisfaction of his predominating instincts.

If he is fat and of average brain capacity he will overcome his physical inertia to the point of securing for himself and his family most of the comforts of modern life.

The average-brained fat man composes a large percentage of our population and the above accounts for his deserved reputation as a generous husband and father.

The Fat Man a Good Provider

¶ The fat man will give his last cent to his wife and children for the things they desire but he is not inclined as much as some other types to hearken to the woes of the world at large. The fat man is essentially a family man, a home man, a respectable, cottage-owning, tax-paying, peaceable citizen.

Not a Reformer

¶ He inclines to the belief that other families, other communities, other classes and other countries should work out their own salvation and he leaves them to do it. In all charitable, philanthropic and community "drives" he gives freely but is not lavish nor sentimental about it. It is often a "business proposition" with him.

When the Fat Man is Poor

¶ Love of ease is the fat man's worst enemy. His inherent contentment, accentuated by the inconvenience of moving about easily or quickly, constantly tempts him to let things slide. When he lacks the brain capacity for figuring out ways and means for getting things easily he is never a great success at anything.

When the extremely fat man's mentality is below the average he often refuses to work—in which case he becomes a familiar figure around public rest rooms, parks and the cheaper hotel lobbies. Such a man finally graduates into the class of professional chair-warmers.

Fat People Love Leisure

¶ A chance to do as we please, especially to do as little hard work as possible, is a secret desire of almost everybody. But the fat man takes the prize for wanting it most.

Not a Strenuous Worker

¶ He is not constructed to work hard like some of the other types, as we shall see in subsequent chapters. His overweight is not only a handicap in that it slows down his movements, but it tends to slow down all his vital processes as well and to overload his heart. This gives him a chronic feeling of heaviness and inertia.

Everybody Likes Him

¶ But Nature must have intended fat people to manage the rest of us instead of taking a hand at the "heavy work." She made them averse to toil and then made them so likable that they can usually get the rest of us to do their hardest work for them.

The World Managed by Fat People

¶ When he is brainy the fat man never stays in the lower ranks of subordinates. He may get a late start in an establishment but he will soon make those *over* him like him so well they will promote him to a chief-clerkship, a foremanship or a managership. Once there he will make those *under* him so fond of him that they will work long and hard for him.

Fat Men to the Top

¶ In this way the fat man of real brains goes straight to the top while others look on and bewail the fact that they do most of the actual work. They fail to recognize that the world always pays the big salaries not for hand work but for head work, and not so much for working yourself as for your ability to get others to work.

The Popular Politician

¶ This capacity for managing, controlling and winning others is what enables this type to succeed so well in politics. The fat man knows how to get votes. He mixes with everybody, jokes with everybody, remembers to ask how the children are—and pretty soon he's the head of his ward. Almost every big political boss is fat.

Makes Others Work

¶ One man is but one man and at best can do little more than a good man-size day of work. But a man who can induce a dozen other man-machines to speed up and turn out a full day's work apiece doesn't need to work his own hands. He serves his employer more valuably as an overseer, foreman or supervisor.

The Fat Salesman

¶ "A fat drummer" is such a common phrase that we would think our ears deceived us did anyone speak of a thin one. Approach five people and say "A traveling salesman," each will tell you that the picture this conjures in his imagination is of a fat, round, roly-poly, good natured, pretty clever man whom everybody likes.

For the fat men are "born salesmen" and they make up a large percentage of that profession. Salesmanship requires mentality plus a pleasing personality. The fat man qualifies easily in the matter of personality. Then he makes little or much money from salesmanship, according to his mental capacity.

The Drummers' Funny Stories

¶ You will note that the conversation of fat people is well sprinkled with funny stories. They enjoy a good joke better than any other type, for a reason which will become more and more apparent to you.

¶ That salesmen are popularly supposed to regale each customer with yarns till he gasps for breath and to get his signature on the dotted line while he is in that weakened condition, is more or less of a myth. It originated from the fact that most salesmen are fat and that fat people tell stories well.

Jokes at Fat Men's Expense

¶ "Look at Fatty," "get a truck," and other jibes greet the fat man on every hand. He knows he can not proceed a block without being the butt of several jokes, but he listens to them all with an amiability surprising to other types.

And this good nature is so apparent that even those who make sport of him are thinking to themselves: "I believe I'd like that man."

The Fat Man's Habits

¶ "Never hurry and never worry" are the unconscious standards underlying many of the reactions of this type. If you will compile a list of the habits of any fat person you will find that they are mostly the outgrowths of one or both of these motives.

Won't Speed Up

¶ You would have a hard time getting an Alimentive to follow out any protracted line of action calling for strenuosity, speed or high tension. He will get as much done as the strenuous man when their mentalities are equal— and often more. The fat person keeps going in a straight line, with uniform and uninterrupted effort, and does not have the blow-outs common to more fidgety people. But hard, fast labor is not in his line.

Loves Comedy

¶ All forms of mental depression are foreign to fat people as long as they are in normal health. We have known a fat husband and wife to be ejected for rent and spend the evening at the movies laughing like four-year-olds at Charlie Chaplin or a Mack Sennett comedy. You have sometimes seen fat people whose financial condition was pretty serious and wondered how they could be so cheerful.

Inclined to Indolence

¶ Fat people's habits, being built around their points of strength and weakness, are necessarily of two kinds—the desirable and the undesirable.

The worst habits of this type are those inevitable to the ease-loving and the immature-minded.

Indolence is one of his most undesirable traits and costs the Alimentive dear.

In this country where energy, push and lightning-like efficiency are at a premium only the fat man of brains can hope to keep up.

The inertia caused by his digestive processes is so great that it is almost insurmountable. The heavy, lazy feeling you have after a large meal is with the fat man interminably because his organism is constantly in the process of digesting large amounts of food.

Likes Warm Rooms

¶ Love of comfort—especially such things as warm rooms and soft beds—is so deeply imbedded in the fiber of this type that he has ever to face a fight with himself which the rest of us do not encounter. This sometimes leads the excessively corpulent person to relax into laziness and slovenliness. An obese individual sometimes surprises us, however, by his ambition and immaculateness.

But such a man or woman almost always combines decided mental tendencies with his alimentiveness.

Enjoys Doing Favors

¶ The habits which endear the fat person to everyone and make us forget his faults are his never-failing hospitality, kindness when you are in trouble, his calming air of contentment, his tact, good nature and the real pleasure he seems to experience when doing you a favor.

His worst faults wreak upon him far greater penalties than fall upon those who associate with him, something that can not be said of the faults of some other types.

Likes Melody

¶ Simple, natural music is a favorite with fat people. Love songs, rollicking tunes and those full of melody are most popular with them. An easy-to-learn, easy-to-sing song is the one a fat man chooses when he names the next selection.

They like ragtime, jazz and music with a swing to it. Music the world over is most popular with fat races. The world's greatest singers and most of its famous musicians have been fat or at least decidedly plump.

Goes to the Cabaret

¶ The fat person will wiggle his toes, tap his fingers, swing his fork and nod his head by the hour with a rumbling jazz orchestra.

When the Alimentive is combined with some other type he will also enjoy other kinds of music but the pure Alimentive cares most for primal tunes and melodies.

Likes a Girly-Show

¶ A pretty-girl show makes a hit with fat women as well as with fat men. Drop into the "Passing Show" and note how many fat people are in the audience. Drop into a theater the next night where a tragedy is being enacted and see how few fat ones are there.

The One Made Sport Of

¶ Fat people enjoy helping out the players, if the opportunity offers. All show people know this.

When one of those tricks is to be played from the foot-lights upon a member of the audience the girl who does it is always careful to select that circular gentleman down front. Let her try to mix up confetti or a toy balloon with a tall skinny man and the police would get a hurry call!

When we describe the bony type you will note how very different he is from our friend the fat man.

A Movie Fan

¶ "The fat man's theater" would be a fitting name for the movie houses of the country. Not that the fat man is the only type patronizing the cinema. The movies cover in one evening so many different kinds of human interests—news, cartoons, features and comedy—that every type finds upon the screen something to interest him.

But if you will do what we have done—stand at the doorway of the leading movie theaters of your city any evening and keep a record of the types that enter you will find the plump are as numerous as all the others combined.

Easy Entertainment

¶ The reason for this is plain to all who are acquainted with Human Analysis: the fat man wants everything the easiest possible way and the movie fulfils this requirement more fully than any other theatrical entertainment. He can drop in when he feels like it and there is no waiting for the show to start, for one thing.

This is a decided advantage to him, for fat people do not like to depend upon themselves for entertainment.

The Babies of the Race

¶ The first stage in biological evolution was the stage in which the alimentary apparatus was developed. To assimilate nutriment was the first function of all life and is so still, since it is the principal requirement for self-preservation.

Being the first and most elemental of our five physiological systems the Alimentive—when it overtops the others—produces a more elemental, infantile nature. The pure Alimentive has rightly been called "the baby of the race." This accounts for many of the characteristics of the extremely fat person, including the fact that it is difficult for him to amuse himself.

He of all types likes most to be amused and very simple toys and activities are sufficient to do it.

Loves the Circus

¶ A serious drama or "problem play" usually bores him but he seldom misses a circus.

The fat person expresses his immaturity also in that he likes to be petted, made over and looked after.

¶ Like the infant he demands food first. Almost the only time a fat man loses his temper is when he has been deprived of his food. The next demand on his list is sleep, another characteristic of the immature.

Give a fat man "three squares" a day and plenty of sleep in a comfortable bed, and he will walk off with the prize for good humor three hundred and sixty-five days in the year. Next to sleep he demands warm clothing in winter and steam heat when the wintry winds blow.

Fat People at the Beach

¶ If it were not for the exertion required in getting to and from the beaches, dressing and undressing, and the momentary coldness of the water, many more Alimentives would go to the beaches in Summer than do.

Not Strenuous

¶ Anything, to be popular with the Alimentive, must be easy to get, easy to do, easy to get away from, easy to drop if he feels like it. Anything requiring the expenditure of great energy, even though it promises pleasure when achieved, is usually passed over by the fat people.

The Art of Getting Out Of It

¶ "Let George do it" is another bit of slang invented by this type. He seldom does anything he really hates to do. He is so likable he either induces you to let him out of it or gets somebody to do it for him. He just naturally avoids everything that is intense, difficult or strenuous.

The Peaceable Type

¶ If an unpleasant situation of a personal or social nature arises—a quarrel, a misunderstanding or any kind of disagreement—the fat man will try to get himself out of it without a discussion.

Except when they have square faces (in which case they are not pure Alimentives), extremely fat people do not mix up in neighborhood, family, church, club or political quarrels. It is too much trouble, for one thing, and for another it is opposed to his peaceable, untensed nature.

Avoids Expensive Quarrels

¶ The fat man has his eye on personal advantages and promotions and he knows that quarrels are expensive, not alone in the chances they lose him, but in nerve force and peace of mind.

The fat man knows instinctively that peace times are the most profitable times and though he is not for "peace at any price" so far as the country is concerned, he certainly is much inclined that way where he is personally concerned. You will be amused to notice how this peace-loving quality increases as one's weight increases. The more fat any individual is the more is he inclined to get what he wants without hostility.

The Real Thing

¶ The favorite "good time" of the Alimentive is one where there are plenty of refreshments. A dinner invitation always makes a hit with him, but beware that you do not lure a fat person into your home and give him a tea-with-lemon wisp where he expected a full meal!

Always Ready for Food

¶ Substantial viands can be served to him any hour of the day or night with the certainty of pleasing him. He loves a banquet, *provided he is not expected to make a speech*. The fat man has a harder time than any other listening to long speeches.

The fashion of trying to mix the two most opposite extremes—food and ideas—and expecting them to go down, was due to our misunderstanding of the real nature of human beings. It is rapidly going out, as must every fashion which fails to take the human instincts into account.

Avoids Sports

¶ No prizes lure a fat man into strenuous physical exercise or violent sports. Although we have witnessed numerous state, national and international tennis, polo, rowing, sprinting, hurdling and swimming contests, we have seen not one player who was fat enough to be included in the pure Alimentive type.

The grand-stands, bleachers and touring cars at these contests contained a generous number of fat people, but their conversation indicated that they were present more from personal interest in some contestant than in the game itself.

The nearest a fat man usually comes to taking strenuous exercise is to drive in an open car. The more easeful that car the better he likes it. He avoids long walks as he would the plague, and catches a street car for a two-block trip.

The Personal Element

¶ Due to his immaturity, the fat person gives little thought to anything save those things which affect him personally.

The calm exterior, unruffled countenance and air of deliberation he sometimes wears, and which have occasionally passed for "judicial" qualities, are largely the results of the fact that the Alimentive refuses to get stirred up over anything that does not concern him personally.

This personal element will be found to dominate the activities, conversation and interests of the Alimentive. For him to like a thing or buy a thing it must come pretty near being something he can eat, wear, live in or otherwise personally enjoy. He confines himself to the concrete and tangible. But most of all he confines himself to things out of which he gets something for himself.

Reading

¶ The fat man is no reader but when he does read it is nearly always something funny, simple or sentimental. In newspapers he reads the "funnies." Magazine stories, if short and full of sentiment, attract him. He seldom reads an editorial and is not a book worm. The newspaper furnishes practically all of the fat man's reading. He seldom owns a library unless he is very rich, and then it is usually for "show."

Avoids Book Stores

¶ In making the investigations for this course, we interviewed many clerks in the bookstores of leading cities throughout the United States. Without exception they stated that few extremely fat people patronized them. "I have been in this store seventeen years and I have never sold a book to a two hundred and fifty pounder," one dealer told us. All this is due to the fact with which we started this chapter—that the fat man is built around his stomach— and stomachs do not read!

Naturally Realistic

¶ The fat man has the child's natural innocence and ignorance of subtle and elusive things. He has the same interest in things and people as does the child; the child's indifference to books, lectures, schools and everything abstract.

Physical Assets

¶ "I believe I could digest nails!" exclaimed a fat friend of ours recently. This perfect nutritive system constitutes the greatest physical superiority of the Alimentive. So highly developed is his whole stomach department that everything "agrees" with him. And everything tends to make him fat.

As Irvin Cobb recently said: "It isn't true that one can't have his cake and eat it, too, for the fat man eats his and keeps it—all."

Physical Liabilities

¶ A tendency to over-eat results naturally from the highly developed eating and digesting system of this type but this in turn overtaxes all the vital organs, as stated before. Also, the fat man's aversion to exercise reduces his physical efficiency.

The pure Alimentive and the alimentively-inclined should learn their normal weight and then keep within it if they desire long lives.

Social Assets

¶ Sweetness of disposition is one of the most valuable of all human characteristics. Fat people possess it more often and more unchangingly than any other type. Other social assets of this type are amenableness, affability, hospitality and approachableness.

Social Liabilities

¶ Gaining his ends by flattery, cajolery, and various more or less innocent little deceptions are the only social handicaps of this type.

Emotional Assets

¶ His unfailing optimism is the most marked emotional quality of this type. Nothing can be so dark that the fat person doesn't find a silver edge somewhere. So in disaster we always send for our fat friends. In the presence of an amply-proportioned individual everything looks brighter. Hope springs eternal in human breasts but the springs are stronger in the plump folks than in the rest of us.

Money spending is also a marked feature of the fat man. His emotions are out-going, never "in-growing." A stingy fat man is unknown.

Emotional Liabilities

¶ A tendency to become spoiled, to pout, and to take out his resentments in babyish ways are the emotional weaknesses of this type. These, as you will note, are the natural reactions of childhood, from which he never fully emerges.

Business Assets

¶ The ability to make people like him is the greatest business and professional asset of this type, and one every other type might well emulate. One average-minded fat man near the door of a business establishment will make more customers in a month by his geniality, joviality and sociableness than a dozen brilliant thinkers will in a year. Every business that deals directly with the public should have at least one fat person in it.

Business Liabilities

¶ A habit of evading responsibility and of "getting out from under" constitutes the inclination most harmful to the business or professional ambitions of this type. Again it is the child in him trying to escape the task set for it and at the same time to avoid punishment.

Domestic Strength

¶ Love of home is a distinguishing domestic trait of all fat people. The fat man's provision for his family is usually as complete as his circumstances will permit and he often stretches it a point.

As parents fat men and women are almost too easy-going for their own future happiness, for they "spoil" their children. But they are more loved by their children than any other type. Being so nearly children themselves they make equals of their children, enter into their games and live their lives with them.

Domestic Weakness

¶ Dependence on others, the tendency of allowing one's self to be supported by brothers or sisters or wife, is the chief domestic weakness of fat people. They should begin early in life to depend upon themselves and make it a practice to carry their share of family responsibilities.

Should Aim At

¶ Developing more of his mental powers with a view to using his head to lessen the manual work he so dislikes, and cultivating an interest in the more mature side of the world in which he lives should be two of the aims of all extremely fat people.

Should Avoid

¶ "Letting down," soft snaps and temptations to evade responsibility should be avoided by the fat. Elbert Hubbard said, "Blessed is the man who is not looking for a soft snap, for he is the only one who shall find it." This explains why the fat man, unless brainy, seldom lands one.

Strongest Points

¶ Optimism, hospitality and harmony are the strongest points in the fat man's nature. Upon them many a man has built a successful life. Without them no individual of any type can hope to be happy.

His popularity and all-around compatibility give the fat man advantages over other types which fairly compensate for the weak cogs in his machinery.

Weakest Points

¶ Self-indulgence of all kinds, over-eating, over-sleeping, under-exercising and the evasion of responsibilities are the weakest points of this type. Despite his many strong points his life is often wrecked on these rocks. He so constantly tends to taking the easy way out. Day by day he gives up chances for ultimate success for the baubles of immediate ease.

He is the most likable of all the types but his indolence sometimes strains even the love of his family to the breaking point.

How to Deal with this Type Socially

¶ Feed him, give him comfortable chairs—the largest you have—and don't drag him into long discussions of any kind. This is the recipe for winning the fat man when you meet him socially.

And whatever you do, don't tell him your troubles! The fat man hates trouble, smothers his own, and you only make him ill at ease when you regale him with yours.

Don't walk him any more than is absolutely necessary. Let him go home early if he starts. He enjoys his sleep and doesn't like to have it interfered with.

¶ Make your conversation deal with concrete personal things and events. Stay away from highbrow subjects. The best places to eat and the best shows of the week are safe subjects to introduce when with very fat people.

How to Deal with this Type in Business

¶ Don't give him hard manual tasks. If you want this kind of work done get some one other than an extremely fat man to do it. If you hire a fat man blame yourself for the result.

Give your fat employee a chance to deal with people in a not-too-serious way, but hold him strictly to the keeping of his records, reports and working hours. If this fat person is a dealer, a merchant or a tradesman keep him to his word. Start out by letting him know you expect the delivery of just what he promises. Don't let him "jolly" you into relinquishing what is rightfully yours. And keep in mind always that the fat person is usually good at heart.

Remember, the chief distinguishing marks of the Alimentive in the order of their importance are ROUNDED OUTLINES, IMMATURE FEATURES and DIMPLED HANDS. A person who has these is largely of the Alimentive type, no matter what other types may be included in his makeup.

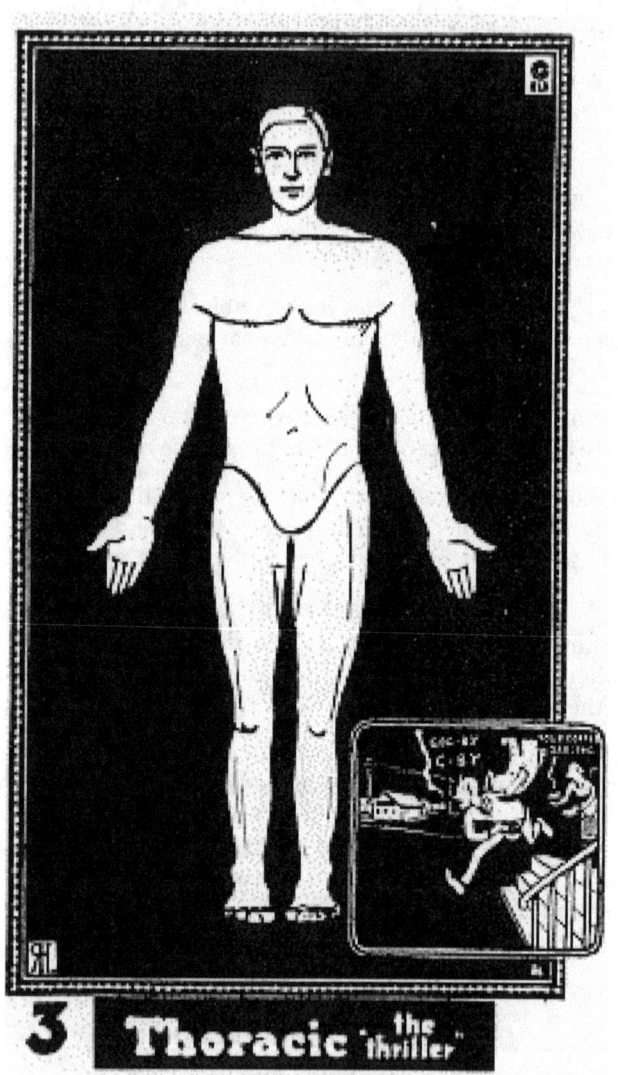

3 **Thoracic** "the thriller"

CHAPTER II

The Thoracic Type

"The Thriller"

 ndividuals in whom the circulatory system (heart, arteries and blood vessels) and the respiratory system (lungs, nose and chest) are more highly developed than any other systems, have been named the Thoracics.

¶ This name comes from the fact that the heart and lungs (which constitute the most important organs of these two closely-allied systems) are housed in the thorax—that little room made by your ribs for the protection of these vital organs.

Physical Resilience
¶ A general elasticity of structure, a suggestion of sinews and physical resilience characterizes this type.

The Florid-Faced, High-Chested Individual
¶ What is known as a "red face," when accompanied by a high chest, always signifies large thoracic tendencies. The high color which in an adult comes and goes is a sure indication of a well developed circulatory system, since high color is caused by the rapid pumping of blood to the tiny blood vessels of the face.

People with little blood, weak hearts or deficient circulation are not florid and must be much overheated or excited to show vivid color in their cheeks.

Betray Their Feelings
¶ On the other hand, the slightest displeasure, enjoyment, surprise or exertion brings the blood rushing to the face and neck of him who has a large, well-developed blood-system. How many times you have heard such a one say: "I am so embarrassed! I flush at every little thing! How I envy the rest of you who come in from a long walk looking so cool!"

The Man of Great Chest Expansion

¶ The largest part of this man's body is around the chest. (See Chart 3) His chest is high for the reason that he has larger lungs than the average.

Advantages of a High Chest

¶ The man of unusual chest-expansion has one great physical asset. The person who breathes deeply has a decided advantage over the man who breathes deficiently. The lungs form the bellows or air-supply for the body's engine, the heart, and with a deficient supply of air the heart does deficient work. Efficient breathing is easy only to the man of large lungs, and only the high chested have large lungs.

Long-Waisted People

¶ A long waist is another thoracic sign, for it is a natural result of the extra house-room required by the large lungs and heart. It is easily detected in both men and women. (See Chart 3)

If you are a close observer you have noticed that some people appear to have a waist line much lower than others; that the belt line dividing the upper part of the body from the lower is proportionately much nearer the floor in some than in others of the same height.

Passing of the "Wasp Waist"

¶ The "straight-up-and-down" lines of today's woman and the slimpsy shoulder-to-heel garments she wears have obliterated her waistline, but you will recall how differently the old "wasp waist" fashions of a score of years ago betrayed the secrets of the short and long waist.

The eighteen-inch belt, of which we were so falsely proud in 1900, told unmistakable facts about milady's thoracic development.

Belts vs. Suspenders

¶ As the tell-tale belt disappeared from woman's wardrobe it appeared in man's, and now betrays the location of his waist with an exactness of which the old-fashioned suspenders were never guilty.

To Test Yourself

¶ If you are a man and have difficulty in getting ready-made coats long enough for you this is certain proof that you have decided thoracic tendencies. If you are a woman who has to forego many a pretty gown because it is not long enough in the waist, the same is true of you.

In women this long waist and high chest give the appearance of small hips and of shoulders a little broader than the average; in men it gives that straight, soldier-like bearing which makes this type of man admired and gazed after as he strides down the street.

The Pure Thoracic Head

¶ A high head is a significant characteristic of the typical Thoracic. (See Chart 4) The Anglo-Saxons tend to have this head and, more than any other races, exhibit thoracic qualities as racial characteristics.

This is considered the handsomest head known. Certainly it lends the appearance of nobility and intelligence. It is not wide, looked at from the front or back, but inclines to be slightly narrower for its height than the Alimentive head.

The Kite-Shaped Face

¶ A face widest through the cheek bones and tapering slightly up the sides of the forehead and downward to the jaw bones is the face of the pure Thoracic. (See Chart 4) This must not be mistaken for the pointed chin nor the pointed head, but is merely a sloping of the face upward and downward from the cheek bones as a result of the unusual width of the nose section. (See Chart 4)

His Well-Developed Nose

¶ The nose section is also high and wide because the typical Thoracic has a nose that is well developed. This is shown not only by its length but by its high bridge.

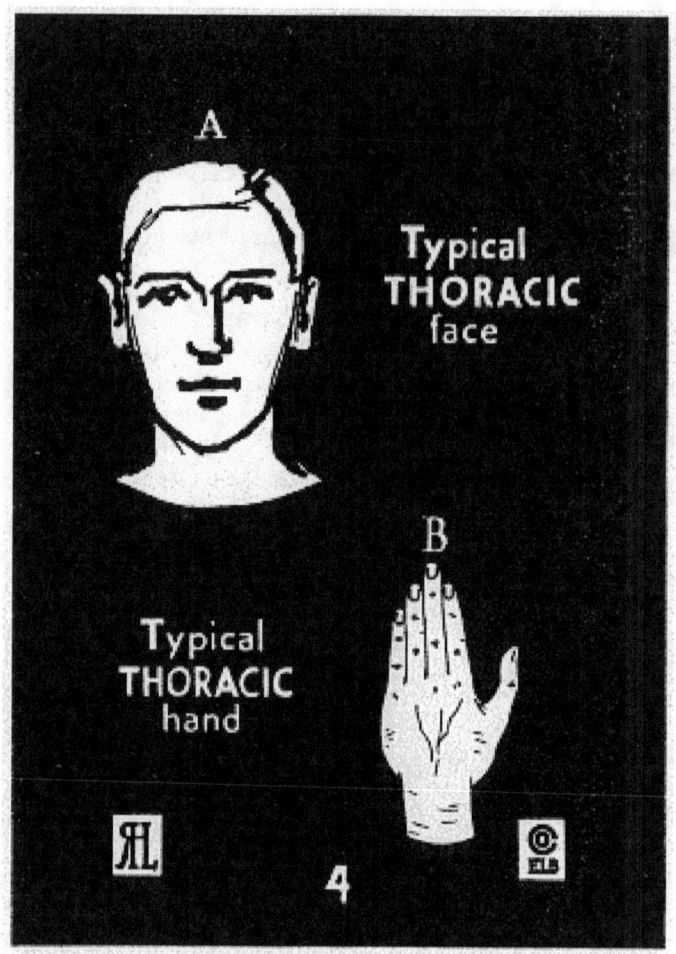

The cause for the width and length of this section is obvious. The nose constitutes the entrance and exit departments of the breathing system. Large lung capacity necessitates a large chamber for the intake and expulsion of air.

Signs of Good Lungs

¶ Whenever you see a man whose face is wide through the cheek bones—with a long, high-bridged open-nostrilled nose—you see a man of good lung capacity and of quick physical energy. When you see any one with pinched nostrils, a face that is narrow through the cheek bones and a low or "sway-back" nose, you see a man whose lung capacity is deficient. Such a person invariably expends his physical energy more slowly.

Freckles, being due to the same causes as red hair and high color, are further indications of thoracic tendencies, though you may belong to this type with or without them.

The Typical Thoracic Hand

¶ The pointed hand is the hand of the pure Thoracic. (See Chart 4) Note the extreme length of the second finger and the pointed effect of this hand when all the fingers are laid together. Any person with a pointed hand such as this has good thoracic development whether it occupies first place in his makeup or not.

The fingers of the Thoracic are also inclined to be more thin-skinned than those of other types.

One may be predominantly Thoracic without these elements but they are indications of the extreme Thoracic type. Naturally the hand of the extreme Thoracic is more pink than the average.

The Beautiful Foot

¶ The Thoracic tends to have more narrow, high-arched feet than other types. As a result this type makes the majority of the beautifully shod.

The Man of Energetic Movements

¶ A hair-trigger nimbleness goes with this type. He is always "poised ready to strike."

All Thoracics use their hands, arms, wrists, limbs and feet alertly and energetically. They open doors, handle implements and all kinds of hand instruments with little blundering. Also their movements are more graceful than those of other types.

The Thoracic Walk

¶ "The springy step" must have been invented to describe the walk of the Thoracic. No matter how hurried, his walk has more grace than the walk of other types. He does not stumble; and it is seldom that a Thoracic steps on the train of his partner's gown.

The Graceful Sitter

¶ The way you sit tells a great deal about your nature. One of the first secrets it betrays is whether you are by nature graceful or ungainly. The person who sits gracefully, who seems to drape himself becomingly upon a chair and to arise from it with ease is usually a Thoracic.

Their excess of energy sometimes gives them the appearance of "fidgeting," but it is an easy, graceful fidget and not as disturbing as that of other types.

Keen Eye and Ear Senses

¶ Quick eyes and keen ears are characteristic of the Thoracics. The millions of stimuli—the sounds, sights and smells impinging every waking moment upon the human consciousness—affect him more quickly and more intensely than any other type. The acuteness of all our senses depends, to a far greater extent than we have hitherto supposed, upon proper heart and lung action.

Take long, deep breaths for five minutes in the open air while walking rapidly enough to make your heart pound, and see how much keener your senses are at the end of that time.

The Thoracic is chronically in this condition because his heart and lungs are going at top speed habitually and naturally all his life.

Susceptible to Heat

¶ Because bodily temperature varies according to the amount of blood and the rapidity of its circulation, this type is always warmer than others. He is extremely susceptible to heat, suffers keenly in warm rooms or warm weather and wears fewer wraps in winter. The majority of bathers at the beaches in summer are largely of this type.

The High-Strung

¶ Nerves as taut as a violin string—due to his acute physical senses and his thin, sensitive skin—plus his instantaneous quickness make the Thoracic what is known as "high-strung."

The Most Temperamental

¶ Because he is keyed to high C by nature, the Thoracic has more of that quality called temperament than any other type.

The wag who said that "temperament was mostly temper" might have reversed it and still have been right. For temper is largely a matter of temperament. Since the Thoracics have more "temperament" it follows naturally that they have more temper, or rather that they show it oftener, just as they show their delightful qualities oftener.

A Continuous Performance

¶ This type, consciously and unconsciously, is a "continuous performance." He is showing you something of himself every moment and if you are interested in human nature, as your reading of this book suggests, you are going to find him a fascinating subject. He is expressing his feelings with more or less abandon all the time and he is likely to express as many as a dozen different ones in as many moments.

The Quick Temper

¶ "Flying off the handle," and "going up in the air" are phrases originally inspired by our dear, delightful friends, the Thoracics.

Other types do these more or less temperamental things but they do not do them as frequently nor on as short notice as this type.

The Human Firefly

¶ A fiery nature is part and parcel of the Thoracic's makeup. But did you ever see a fiery-natured man who didn't have lots of warm friends! It is the grouch—in whom the fire starts slowly and smoulders indefinitely—that nobody likes. But the man who flares up, flames for a moment and is calm the next never lacks for companions or devotees.

The Red-Haired

¶ One may belong to the Thoracic type whether his hair is blonde or brunette or any of the shades between, but it is an interesting fact that most of the red-haired are largely of this type. "He didn't have red hair for nothing" is a famous phrase that has been applied to the red-haired, quick-tempered Thoracic for generations.

You will be interested to note that this high color and high chest are distinctly noticeable in most of the red-haired people you know—certain proof that they approximate this type.

As you walk down the street tomorrow look at the people ahead of you and when you find a "red-head" notice how much more red his neck is than the necks of the people walking beside him. This flushed skin almost always accompanies red hair, showing that most red-haired people belong to this type.

The "Flash in the Pan"

¶ The red-haired man's temper usually expends itself instantly. His red-hot fieriness is over in a moment. But for every enemy he has two friends— friends who like his flame, even though in constant danger from it themselves.

Whereas the Alimentive avoids you if he disagrees with you, the Thoracic likes to tell you in a few hot words just what he thinks of you. But the chances are that he will be so completely over it by lunch time that he will invite you out with him.

Desire for Approbation

¶ To be admired and a wee bit envied are desires dear to the heart of this type. Everybody, to a greater or lesser degree, desires these things, but to no other type do they mean so much as to this one. We know this because no other type, in any such numbers, takes the trouble or makes the sacrifices necessary to bring them about.

Acts Indicate Desires

¶ The ego of every individual craves approval but the majority of the other types craves something else more—the particular something in each case depending upon the type to which the individual belongs.

You can always tell what any individual WANTS MOST by what he DOES. The man who *thinks* he wants a thing or wishes he wanted it talks about getting it, envies those who have it and *plans* to start doing something about it. But the man who really WANTS a thing GOES AFTER it, sacrifices his leisure, his pleasures and sometimes love itself—and GETS it.

Shines in Public Life

¶ The lime-light appeals more to this type than to others because it goes further toward gratifying his desire for approbation. So while other men and women are dreaming of fame the Thoracic practises, ploughs and pleads his way to it.

The personal adulation of friends and of the multitude is the breath of life to him. Extremes of this type consider no self-denial too great a price to pay for it.

Many on the Stage

¶ The stage in all its forms is as natural a field to the Thoracic as salesmanship is to the Alimentive. The pleas of fond papas and fearsome mamas are usually ineffective with this type of boy or girl when he sets his heart on a career before the foot-lights or in the movies.

Whether they achieve it or not will depend on other, and chiefly mental, traits in each individual's makeup, but the yearning for it in some form is always there. So the managers' waiting rooms are always crowded with people of this type. It is this intensity of desire which has goaded and inspired most stage artists on to success in their chosen fields.

"Put Yourself in His Place"

¶ To be able to put one's self in the role of another, to feel as he feels; to be so keenly sensitive to his situation and psychology that one almost becomes that person for the time being, is the heart and soul of acting.

The Thoracic has this sensitiveness naturally. After long study and acquaintance you may be able to put yourself in the place of a few friends. The Thoracic does this instantly and automatically.

Tendency, Not Toil, Makes Fame

¶ Those who have succeeded to fame in any given line are wont to proclaim, "Hard work is the secret of success," and to take great credit unto themselves for the labor they have expended on their own.

It is true of course that all success entails hard work. But the man or woman sufficiently gifted to rise to the heights gets from that gift such a strong inward urge towards its expression that what he does in that direction is not work to him. The long hours, concentration and study devoted to it are more pleasurable than painful to him. He chooses such activities voluntarily.

Nature the Real Artist

¶ Nothing can rightly be called work which one does out of sheer preference. Work never made an actress and work never made a singer where innate talent for these arts was lacking. Nature, the true maker of every famous name, bestows ninety per cent and man, if he hustles, can provide the other very necessary ten. But his sense of humor if not his sense of justice should be sufficient to prevent his trying to rob the Almighty of His due.

Success for All

¶ Every individual who is not feeble-minded can be a success at something in this big world. Every normal-minded individual is able to create, invent, improve, organize, build or market some of the myriads of things the world is crying for. But he will succeed at only those things in which his physiological and psychological mechanisms perform their functions easily and naturally.

Why We Work

¶ Man is, by inclination, very little of a worker. He is, first, a wanter—a bundle of instincts; second, a feeler—a bundle of emotions; last and least, he is a thinker. What real work he does is done not because he likes it but because it serves one of these first two bundles of instincts.

When the desire for leisure is stronger than the other urges, leisure wins. But in all ambitious men and women the desire for other things outweighs the leisure-urge.

Ambition and Type

¶ Now what is it that causes some to have ambition and others to lack it?

Your ambitions take the form determined by your predominating physiological system. For instance, in every great singer the Thoracic has been present either as the first or second element.

The effect of the physical upon our talents is no more marked anywhere than here. For it is his unusual lung power, his high chest, the sounding boards in his nose section and his superior vocal cords that make the real foundation of every singer's fame. These physiological conditions are found in extreme degree only in persons of thoracic tendencies.

It was the great lung-power of Caruso that made him a great singer. It was his remarkable heart-power that brought him through an illness in February, 1921, when every newspaper in the world carried on its front page the positive statement that he could not live another day. That he lived for six months afterward was due chiefly to his remarkable heart.

The nature resulting from a large heart and large lungs is one distinctly different from all others—in short, the Thoracic nature.

The Best Dressed

¶ The best dressed man and the best dressed woman in your town belong predominantly to this type. This is no accident. The Thoracics, being possessed of acute eye senses, are more sensitive to color and line than any other type. These are the foundations of "style" and artistic grooming.

Clothes Can Unmake the Man

¶ Being desirous of the approval of others and realizing that though clothes do not make the man they can unmake him, this type looks to his laurels on this point.

Because clothes determine the first impressions we make upon strangers and because that impression is difficult to change, clothes are of vast importance in this maze of human relationships.

The Thoracic is more sensitive to the attitude of others because their attitude is more vital to his self-expression. He senses from childhood the bearing that clothes have for or against him in the opinion of others and how they can aid him to express his personality.

The Glass of Fashion

¶ The Thoracic therefore often becomes "the glass of fashion and the mold of form." His consciousness of himself is so keen that, even when alone, he prefers those things in dress which are at once fine, fancy and fashionable.

Some types are indifferent to clothes, some ignorant of clothes and some defiant in their clothes but the Thoracic always has a keen sense of fitness in the matter of apparel.

Distinction in Dress

¶ The distinctive dresser is one who essays the extremely fashionable, the "last moment" touch. He is always a step or two ahead of the times. His ties, handbags, handkerchiefs and stick pins are "up to the minute." Such a man or woman invariably has a large thoracic development and is well repaid by the public for his pains.

Dress the Universal Language

¶ The public looks more eagerly than we suppose to changes in styles and fads. It gives, in spite of itself, instantaneous admiration of a sort to those who follow the dictates of fashion. This being one of the quickest roads to adulation, it is often utilized by this type.

The Newest in Hairdressing

¶ The latest thing in coiffures is always known by the Thoracic woman. And because she is, more often than any other type, a beautiful woman she can wear her hair in almost any style and find it becoming.

So when puffs were the thing this type of woman not only wore puffs but the most extreme and numerous puffs. When the "sticking-to-the-face" style was in vogue she bought much bandoline and essayed the sleekest and shiniest head of all. When the ear-bun raged she changed those same paper-like curls over night into veritable young sofa cushions.

Always on "Dress Parade"

¶ With intent to keep the spotlight on himself the Thoracic is always on dress parade. He is vividly aware of himself; he knows what kind of picture he is making. He is seldom "self-conscious," in the sense of being timid. When he does happen to be timid he suffers, by reason of his greater desire for approval, more acutely than any other type.

Affectability His Keynote

¶ Instantaneous reaction to stimuli—with all the reflex actions resulting therefrom—constitutes the keynote of this type. This makes an individual who is physiologically and psychologically affectable.

Because life is full of all kinds of stimuli, acting during every waking moment upon every sense in the organism, any person who is high strung finds himself in the midst of what might be called "nerve-bedlam."

Gets the Most Out of Everything

¶ Because of this same highly sensitized makeup the Thoracic gets more sensations out of every incident than the rest of us do. He experiences more joy in the space of a lifetime but also more disappointment.

The Human Violin

¶ For the same reason that the violin vibrates to a greater number of sounds than the organ, the Thoracic is a more vibrant individual than others. He is impelled to an expressiveness of voice, manner and action that often looks like pretence to less impulsive people. In other types it would be, but to the Thoracic it is so natural and normal that he is often much surprised to hear that he has the reputation of being "affected."

A Reputation for Flightiness

¶ This lightning-like liveliness of face, body and voice, his quick replies and instantaneous reactions to everything also cause him to be called "flighty."

The Quick Thinker

¶ We are prone to judge every one by ourselves. People whose mental or physical senses are less "keyed-up," less sensitive, call the Thoracic "rattle-brained."

Usually such a man's brain is not rattled at all; it is working, as all brains do in response to the messages reaching it, via the telegraph wires of the five senses.

In the Thoracic these wires happen to be more taut than in the other types. He gets sensations from sights, sounds, tastes, touches and smells much more quickly than the rest of us do. These messages are sent to the brain more rapidly and, since sensation is responsible for much of our thinking, this man's brain thinks a little more speedily than that of other types.

It does not necessarily think any better. Often it does need slowing down. But compared to the thought-power of some of the other types the Thoracic's speed makes up for much of his carelessness. He makes more mistakes in judgment than other types but can "right-about-face" so quickly he usually remedies them while other types are still trying to decide when to start.

To hold himself back is the hardest lesson for this type to learn.

His Changeability

¶ This tendency to let himself go brings the Thoracic a great deal of unhappiness and failure. He plunges so quickly that he often fails to take into consideration the various elements of the situation.

His physical senses tell him a thing should be done and rush him headlong into actions that he knows are ill-advised the moment he has time to think them over. In turning around and righting his mistakes he often hears himself called "changeable" and "vacillating."

His "Batting Average"

¶ In this, as in other things, we have a tendency toward smugness, shortsightedness and egotism. The man who makes but one mistake a year because he makes but two decisions is wrong fifty per cent of the time. Yet he self-satisfiedly considers himself superior to the Thoracic because he has caught the latter in six "poor deals within six months." At the rate the average Thoracic acts this would be about one mistake in a thousand—a much "better batting average" than the other man's.

But because the confidence of others in our stability is of prime importance to us all, this type or any one inclined to definite thoracic tendencies should take pains to prevent this impression from settling into the minds of his friends.

Should Get Onto the Highway

¶ The greatest reason for striving toward stability in action and more slowness in decision, however, is for his own future's sake. The man who is constantly making decisions and being compelled to alter them gets nowhere. He may have the best engine and the finest car in the world but if he runs first down this by-path, and then that, he will make little progress on the main highway.

Should Have an Aim

¶ An aim, a definite goal is essential to the progress of any individual. It should be made with care and in keeping with one's personality, talents, training, education, environment and experience, and having been made should be adhered to with the determination which does not permit little things to interfere with it.

Eliminating Non-Essentials

¶ The big problem of individual success is the problem of eliminating non-essentials—of "hewing to the line, letting the chips fall where they may." Most of the things that steal your time, strength, money and energy are nothing but chips. If you pay too much attention to them you will never hew out anything worth while.

No Vain Regrets

¶ If you are a Thoracic don't regret the fact that you are not a one-decision-a-year man, but try to make fewer and better decisions.

Your quickness, if called into counsel, will enable you to see from what instincts your mistakes habitually arise and the direction in which most of them have pointed. And you will see this with so much greater dispatch than the average person that you will lose little time.

You should begin today to analyze your most common errors in judgment that you may guard against their recurrence.

Always Slightly Thrilled

¶ Even when apparently composed the Thoracic is always a wee bit thrilled. Everything he sees, hears, touches, tastes or smells gives him such keen sensations that he lives momentarily in some kind of adventure.

He languishes in an unchanging environment and finds monotony almost unbearable.

Lights and Shadows

¶ "Never two minutes the same" fitly describes this type. He passes rapidly from one vivid sensation to another and expresses each one so completely that he is soon ready for the next. He has fewer complexes than any other type because he does not inhibit as much.

The Uncorked Bottle

¶ The "lid" is always off of the Thoracic. This being the case he suffers little from "mental congestion" though he sometimes pays a high price for his self-expression.

Everybody is Interesting

¶ Most of us are much more interesting than the world suspects. But the world is not made up of mind readers. We keep our most interesting thoughts and the most interesting side of ourselves hidden away. Even your dearest friends are seldom given a peep into the actual You. And this despite the fact that we all recognize this as a deficiency in others.

We bottle up ourselves and defy the world's cork-screws—all save the Thoracic. He allows his associates to see much of what is passing in his mind all the time. Because we are all interested in the real individual and not in masks this type usually is much sought after.

Not Secretive

¶ The Thoracic does not by preference cover up; he does not by preference secrete; he does not, except when necessary, keep his plans and ways dark. He is likely to tell not only his family but his newest acquaintances just what he is planning to do and how he expects to do it.

The naturally secretive person who vaguely refers to "a certain party" when he has occasion to speak of another is the exact opposite of this type.

His "Human Interest"

¶ We are all interested in the little comings and goings of our friends. Upon this fact every magazine and newspaper builds its "human interest" stories. We may be indifferent to what the President of the United States is doing about international relations but what he had for breakfast is mighty interesting. Few people read inaugural addresses, significant though they often are to the world and to the reader himself. But if the President would write ten volumes on "Just How I Spend My Sundays," it would be a "best seller."

Naturally Confidential

¶ Personal experiences, personal secrets and personal preferences are subjects we are all interested in. These are the very things with which the Thoracic regales his friends and about which he is more frank and outspoken than any other type. He makes many friends by his obvious openness and his capacity for seeing the interesting details which others overlook.

Charming Conversationalist

¶ Colorful, vivid words and phrases come easily to the tongue of this type for he sees the unusual, the fascinating, in everything. Since any one can make a thing interesting to others if he is really interested in it himself, the Thoracic makes others see and feel what he describes. He is therefore known as the most charming conversationalist.

Beautiful Voice

¶ The most beautiful voices belong to people who are largely of this type. This is due, as we have said before, to physiological causes. The high chest, sensitive vocal cords, capacious sounding boards in the nose and roof of the mouth all tend to give the voice of the Thoracic many nuances and accents never found in other types.

His pleasing voice plus the vividness of his expressions and his lack of reticence in giving the intimate and interesting details are other traits which help to make the Thoracic a lively companion.

The Lure of Spontaneity

¶ The most beloved people in the world are the spontaneous. We lead such drab lives ourselves and keep back so much, we like to see a little Niagara of human emotion occasionally. The Thoracic feels everything keenly. Life's experiences make vivid records on the sensitive plate of his mind. He puts them on the Victrola that is himself and proceeds to run them off for your entertainment.

Sometimes a "Bubbler"

¶ "A constant stream of talk" must have been first said in describing this type. For while others are carefully guarding their real feelings and thoughts the Thoracic goes merrily on relieving himself of his.

More sedate and somber types call the Thoracics "bubblers" or "spouters" just for this reason.

The Incessant Talker

¶ "That person's talk gets on my nerves," is a remark often made by one of the staid, stiff types concerning the seldom silent, extremely florid individual. So natural is this to the Thoracic that he is entirely unconscious of the wearing effect he has on other people.

A Sense of Humor

¶ Seeing the funny side of everything is a capacity which comes more naturally to this type than to others. This is due to the psychological fact that nothing is truly humorous save what is slightly "out of plumb."

Real humor lies in detecting and describing that intangible quirk. No type has the sensitiveness essential to this in any such degree as the Thoracic. Individuals of other types sometimes possess a keen sense of humor. This trait is not confined to the Thoracic. But it is a significant fact that almost every humorist of note has had this type as the first or second element in his makeup.

The Human Fireworks

¶ "He is a skyrocket," or "she is a firefly," are phrases often used to describe that vivacious individual whose adeptness at repartee puts the rest of the crowd in the background. These people are always largely or purely Thoracic. They never belong predominately to the fourth type.

The next time you find such a person note how his eyes flash, how his color comes and goes and the many indescribable gradations of voice which make him the center of things.

"He is always shooting sparks," said a man recently in describing a florid, high-chested friend.

Never Dull Company

¶ His "line" may not interest you but the Thoracic himself is usually interesting. He is an actual curiosity to the quiet, inexpressive people who never can fathom how he manages to talk so frankly and so fast.

Such a person is seldom dull. He is everything from a condiment to a cocktail and has the same effect on the average group of more or less drab personalities.

Lives in the Heights and Depths

¶ "Glad one moment and sad the next" is the way the ticker would read if it could make a record of the inner feelings of the average Thoracic. These feelings often come and go without his having the least notion of what causes them. Ordinarily these unaccountable moods are due to sensations reaching his subconscious mind, of which no cognizance is taken by his conscious processes.

Called "Intuitive"

¶ This ability to "get" things, to respond quickly with his physical reactions while devoting his mental ones to something else, has obtained for this type the reputation of possessing more "intuition" than others.

Source of "Hunches"

¶ That there is no such thing as intuition in the old sense of getting a "hunch" from the outside is now agreed by psychologists. The thing we have called intuition, they maintain, is not due to irregular or supernatural causes but to our own normal natural mental processes.

The impression that he gets this knowledge or suspicion from the outside is due, the scientists say, to the fact that his thinking has proceeded at such lightning-like speed that he was unable to watch the wheels go round. The only thing of which he is conscious is the final result or sum at the bottom of the column called his "hunch." He is not aware of the addition and subtraction which his mind went through to get it for him.

Easily Excited

¶ "Off like a shot" is a term often applied to the Thoracic. He is the most easily excited of all types but also the most easily calmed. He recovers from every mood more quickly and more completely than other types. Under the influence of emotion he often does things for which he is sorry immediately afterward.

On the Spur of the Moment

¶ This type usually does a thing quickly or not at all. He is a gun that is always cocked. So he hits a great many things in the course of a lifetime and leads the most exciting existence of any type. Being able to get thrills out of the most commonplace event because of seeing elements in it which others overlook, he finds in everyday life more novelty than others ever see.

The Adventurers

¶ Romance and adventure always interest this type. He lives for thrills and novel reactions and usually spares no pains or money to get them. A very slangy but very expressive term used frequently by these people is, "I got a real kick out of that."

This craving for adventure, suspense and zest often lures this type into speculation, gambling and various games of chance. The danger in flying, deep-sea diving, auto-racing and similar fields has a strong appeal for this type—so strong that practically every man or woman who follows these professions is of this type.

Tires of Sameness

¶ The Thoracic soon tires of the same suit, the same gown, the same house, the same town and even the same girl. He wrings the utmost out of each experience so quickly and so completely that he is forever on the lookout for new worlds to conquer. Past experiences are to him as so many lemons out of which he has taken all the juice. He anticipates those of the future as so many more to be utilized in the same way.

Likes Responsive People

¶ We all like answers. We want to be assured that what we have said or done has registered. The Thoracic is always saying or doing something and can't understand why other people are so unresponsive. He is as responsive as a radio wire. Everything hits the mark with him and he lets you know it. So, naturally, he enjoys the same from others and considers those less expressive than himself stiff, formal or dull.

The kind of person the Thoracic likes best is one sufficiently like himself to nod and smile and show that he fully understands but who will not interrupt his stream of talk.

People He Dislikes

¶ The stolid, indifferent or cold are people the Thoracic comes very near disliking. Their evident self-complacency and immobility are things he does not understand at all and with which he has little patience.

Such people seem to him to be cold, unfeeling, almost dead. So he steers clear of them. It was surely a Thoracic who first called these people "sticks." But the reason for their acting like sticks will be apparent in another chapter.

His Pet Aversions

¶ Whereas the Alimentive avoids people he does not care for, the Thoracic is inclined to betray his aversions. He occasionally delights to put people he dislikes at a disadvantage by his wit or satire. The stony individual who walks through life like an Ionian pillar is a complete mystery to the Thoracic; and the pillar returns the compliment. We do not like anything we do not understand and we seldom understand anything that differs decidedly from ourselves.

Thus we distrust and dislike foreigners, and to a greater or lesser extent other families, people from other sections of the country, etc. The Easterner and Westerner have a natural distrust of each other; and the Civil War is not the only reason for the incompatibility of Southerners and Northerners.

So it is with individuals. Those who differ too widely in type never understand each other. They have too little of the chief thing that builds friendships— emotions in common.

The Forgiving Man

¶ If you have once been a real friend of a Thoracic and a quarrel comes between you, he may be ever so bitter and biting in the moment of his anger but in most cases he will forgive you eventually.

Really Forgets Disagreements

¶ It is not as easy for other types to forgive; they often refrain from attempting a reconciliation. But the Thoracic's forgiveness is not only spontaneous but genuine.

The Alimentive bears no grudges because it is too much trouble. The Thoracic finds it hard to maintain a grudge because he gets over it just as he gets over everything else. His anger oozes away or he wakes up some fine morning and finds, like the boy recovering from the chickenpox, that he "simply hasn't it any more."

Diseases He is Most Susceptible To

¶ Acute diseases are the ones chiefly affecting this type. Everything in his organism tends to suddenness and not to sameness.

Just as he is inclined to get into and out of psychological experiences quickly, so he is inclined to sudden illnesses and to sudden recuperations. A Thoracic seldom has any kind of chronic ailment. If he acquires a superabundance of avoirdupois he is in danger of apoplexy. The combination of extreme Thoracic and extreme Alimentive tendencies is the cause of this disease.

Likes Fancy Foods

¶ Variety and novelty in food are much enjoyed by this type. The Alimentive likes lots of rich food but he is not so desirous of varieties or freak dishes. But the Thoracic specializes in them.

You can not mention any kind of strange new dish whose investigation won't appeal to some one in the crowd, and that person is always somewhat thoracic. It gives him another promise of "newness."

Foreign dishes of all kinds depend for their introduction into this country almost entirely upon these florid patrons. According to the statements of restauranteurs this type says, "I will try anything once." Many-course dinners, if the food is good, are especially popular with them.

"The Trimmings" at Dinner

¶ Out-of-the-ordinary surroundings in which to dine are always welcome to this type. The hangings, pictures, and furniture mean much to him. Most people like music at meals but to the Thoracic it is almost indispensable. He is so alive in every nerve, so keyed-up and has such intense capacity for enjoyment of many things simultaneously that he demands more than other types. An attentive waiter who ministers to every movement and anticipates every wish is also a favorite with the Thoracic when out for dinner.

Sensitive to His Surroundings

¶ Colorful surroundings are more necessary to the Thoracic than to other types. The ever-changing fashions in house decorations are welcome innovations to him. He soon grows tired of a thing regardless of how much he liked it to begin with.

Take notice amongst your friends and you will see that the girl who changes the furniture all around every few weeks is invariably of this type. "It makes me feel that I have changed my location and takes the place of a trip," explained one girl not long ago.

Wants "Something Different"

¶ The exact color of hangings, wall-paper, interior decorations and accessories are matters of vital import to this type. Whereas the Alimentives demand comfort, the Thoracics ask for "something different," something that catches and holds the eye—that makes an instantaneous impression upon the onlooker and gives him one more thing by which to remember the personality of the one who lives there.

This type considers his room and home as a part of himself and takes the pains with them which he bestows upon his clothes.

When He is Rich

¶ Wealth to the Thoracic means unlimited opportunity for achieving the unusual in everything. His tastes are more extravagant than those of other types. Uncommon works of art are usually found in the homes of this type. The most extraordinary things from the most extraordinary places are especial preferences with him.

He carries out his desire for attention here as in everything else and what he buys will serve that end directly or indirectly.

Fashion and "Flare"

¶ "Flare" aptly describes the quality which the pure Thoracic desires in all that touches him and his personality. It must have verve and "go" and distinctiveness. It must be "the latest" and "the thing."

He is the last type of all to submit to wearing last year's suit, singing last year's songs, or driving in a last year's model.

Likes Dash

¶ The Thoracic wants everything he wears, drives, lives in or owns to "get across," to make an impression. The fat man loves comfort above all else, but the florid man loves distinction.

He does not demand such easy-to-wear garments as the fat man. On the contrary, he will undergo extreme discomfort if it gives him a distinctive appearance. He wants his house to be elegant, the grounds "different," the view unusual.

Has Color Sense

¶ Whereas the fat man when furnishing a home devotes his attention to soft beds, steam heat and plenty of cushioned divans, the Thoracic thinks of the chandeliers, the unusual chairs, the pretty front doorstep, the landscape gardening and the color schemes.

When He is in Moderate Circumstances

¶ When only well to do this type will be found to have carried out furnishings and decorations with the taste worthy of much larger purses. When merely well to do he wears the very best clothes he can possibly afford, and often a good deal better. This type does not purpose to be outwitted by life. He tries always to put up a good showing.

When He is Poor

¶ The Thoracic is seldom poor. He has so much personality, ginger and go of the sort that is required in the world of today that he usually has a good position. He may not like the position. But in spite of the fact that he finds it harder to tolerate disagreeable things than any other type, he will endure it for he knows that the rewards he is after can not be had by the down-and-outer.

The natural and normal vanity of the Thoracic stands him in hand here more than in almost any other place in life.

The World Entertained by Them

¶ Behind every row of foot-lights you will find more people of this type than any other. The Alimentive manages the world but the Thoracic entertains it.

He comprises more of the dancers, actors, operatic stars and general entertainers than any other two types combined. In everything save acrobatics and oratory he holds the platform laurels.

As already pointed out, his adaptability, spontaneity and love of approval are responsible for this.

His Fastidious Habits

¶ The Thoracic is the most fastidious of all the types. His thin skin and sensitive nerves make him more conscious of roughness and slovenliness than others. The result is that he is what is called "more particular" about his person than are other types. The fat man often wears an old pair of shoes long past their usefulness, but the florid man thinks more of the impression he creates than of his own personal comfort, and will wear the shiniest of patent leathers on the hottest day if they are the best match for his suit.

Likes All Music

¶ Every kind of music is enjoyed by the pure Thoracic because he experiences so many moods.

Entertainment He Prefers

¶ Social affairs of an exclusive order where he wears his "best bib and tucker" and everybody else does the same, are amongst the favorite diversions of this type. He makes a favorable impression under such conditions and is well aware of it.

Other reasons for this preference are his brilliant conversational powers, his charm and his enjoyment of other people and their view-points. The Thoracic is also exceedingly fond of dancing.

Enjoys Vaudeville

¶ The average Thoracic enjoys vaudeville, Follies, revues, etc., because they are full of quick changes of program. He enjoys, as does every type, certain kinds of movies, but he constitutes no such percentage of the movie-going audience as some other types.

Reading

¶ Books and stories that are romantic, adventurous, and different are the favorites of this type. Detective stories are often in high favor with him also.

Physical Assets

¶ The physical advantages of this type are his quick energy—based on his wonderful breathing system—and the rich, rapid-flowing blood, produced by his wonderful heart system.

He is noted for his ability to get "his second wind" and has remarkable capacity for rising to sudden physical emergencies.

Physical Liabilities

¶ A tendency to over-excitement and the consequent running down of his batteries is a physical pitfall often fatal to this type.

Favorite Sports

¶ Hurdling, sprinting, tennis and all sports requiring short, intense spurts of energy are the ones in which this type excels.

Social Assets

¶ Charm and responsiveness are the chief social assets of the Thoracic. Inasmuch as these are the most valuable of all social traits, he has a better natural start in human relationships than any other type.

Social Liabilities

¶ Quick temper, his inflammable nature and appearances of vanity are his greatest social liabilities. They stand between him and success many times. He must learn to control them if he desires to reap the full benefit of his remarkable assets.

Emotional Assets

¶ Instantaneous sympathy and the lack of poisonous inhibitions are the outstanding emotional assets of this type.

Emotional Liabilities

¶ Impatience, mercurial emotions and the expenditure of too much of his electricity in every little experience are the tendencies most to be guarded against.

Business Assets

¶ That he is a "good mixer" and has the magnetism to interest and attract others are his most valuable business traits.

Business Liabilities

¶ An appearance of flightiness and his tendency to hop from one subject to another, stand in the way of the Thoracic's promotion many times.

Domestic Strength

¶ The ability to entertain and please his own family and to give of himself to them as freely as he gives himself to the world at large, is one of the most lovable thoracic traits.

Domestic Weakness

¶ The temperament and temper of this type constitute a real domestic problem for those who live with them. But they are so forgiving themselves that it is almost impossible to hold anything against them.

Should Aim At

¶ The Thoracic should aim at making fewer decisions, at finishing what he starts, and of wasting less energy in unnecessary words and motions.

Should Avoid

¶ All situations, conditions and people who "Slip the belt off the will," who tend to cut life up into bits by dissipation or pleasure-seeking, should be avoided by this type because they aggravate his own weaknesses in that direction.

Strong Points

¶ Personal ambition, adaptability and quick physical energy are the strongest points of the Thoracic.

Weakest Points

¶ Too great excitability, irresponsibility and supersensitiveness, are the weakest points of this type.

How to Deal with This Type Socially

¶ Give him esthetic surroundings, encourage him to talk, and respond to what he says. These are the certain methods for winning him in social intercourse.

How to Deal with this Type in Business

¶ Get his name on the dotted line NOW, or don't expect it. If he is an employee let him come into direct contact with people, give his personality a chance to get business for you, don't forget to praise him when deserved, and don't pin him down to routine. This type succeeds best in professions where his personal charm can be capitalized, and does *not* belong in any strictly commercial business.

Remember, the chief distinguishing marks of the Thoracic in the order of their importance, are FLUSHED COMPLEXION, HIGH CHEST and LONG WAIST. Any person who has these is largely of the Thoracic type, no matter what other types may be included in his makeup.

CHAPTER III

The Muscular Type

"The Worker"

eople in whom the muscular system is proportionately larger and more highly developed than any of their other systems are Musculars. This system consists of the muscles of the organism.

The "Lean Meat" Type

¶ The muscle-system of the human body is simply a co-ordinated, organized arrangement of layers of lean meat, of which every individual has a complete set.

An individual's muscles may be small, flabby, deficient in strength or so thin as to be almost imperceptible but they are always there—elementary in the infant, full grown in the adult and remnants in the aged. But they are so smoothly fitted together, so closely knitted and usually so well covered that we seldom realize their complexity or importance.

In the pure Muscular type his muscles are firm and large. Such muscles can not be disguised but seem to stand out all over him.

Helpless Without Them

¶ Without them we would be helpless masses of fat and bone; we could not blink an eye nor lift a finger. Yet we are so accustomed to them that we rarely think of them and seldom give them credit for what they do.

Without their wonder-work to adjust the eyes we could not see; without their power the heart would cease to beat. We can not smile, sob, speak nor sing without using them. We would have no pianists, violinists, dancers, aviators, inventors or workers of any kind without them.

Everything we put together—from hooks and eyes to skyscrapers—is planned by our brains but depends for its materialization upon the muscles of the human body.

How to Know Him

¶ Look at any individual and you will note one of these three conditions: that his bones seem to be covered just by skin and sinews (which means that he belongs to the fourth type) or thickly padded with fat (in which case he is largely of the first type) or well upholstered with *firm* meat.

In the latter case he is largely Muscular, no matter what other types may be present in his makeup.

In a short time you will be able to tell, at a glance, whether the padding on an individual is mostly fat or mostly muscle, because fat is always round and soft while muscle is firm and definite.

Physical Solidity

¶ A general solidity of structure, as distinguished from the softness of the Alimentive and the resilience of the Thoracic, characterizes the Muscular. (See Chart 5)

Poke your finger into a fat man's hand and though it makes a dent that dent puffs back quickly. Do the same to the Muscular and you will find a firmness and toughness of fiber that resists but stays there longer once the dent is made.

Not So Malleable

¶ This little illustration is typical of the differences between these two natures throughout their entirety. Just as the fat man's face gives to your touch, *he* will give in to you more easily than any other type; but he will go back to the same place sooner and more smoothly when your pressure is removed.

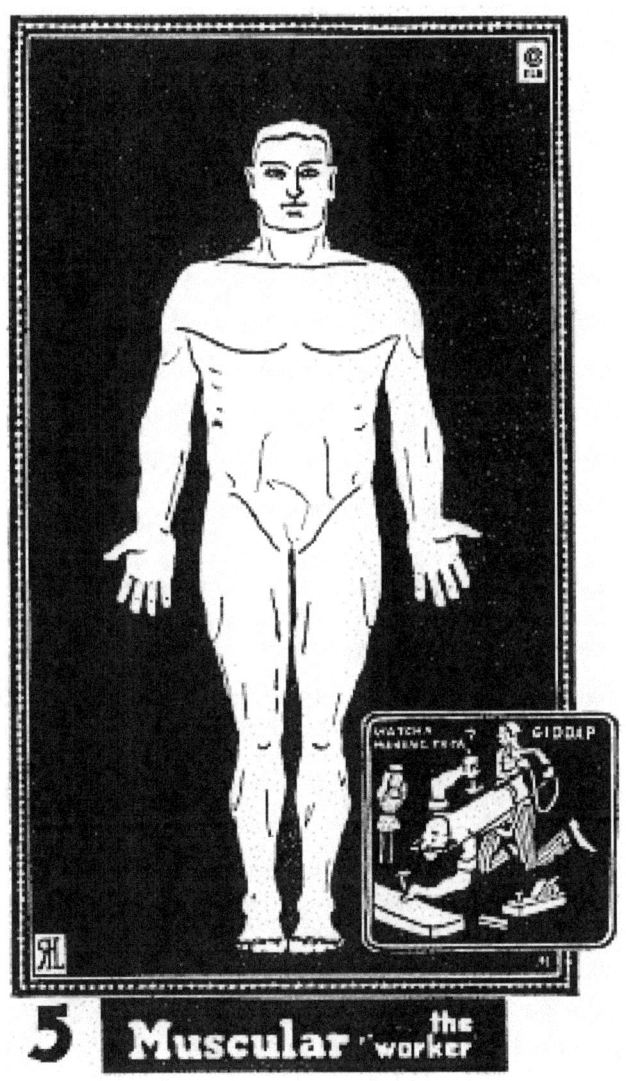

5 Muscular the worker

The Muscular does not mold so easily, is less suggestible, is less tractable than the Alimentive or Thoracic but is less likely to revert afterwards.

Built on the Square

¶ "On the Square" is a figurative expression usually applying to a moral tendency. In this sense it is as often possessed by one type as another. But in a purely literal sense the Muscular is actually built on the square. His whole figure is a combination of squares.

The Alimentive is built upon the circle, the Thoracic on the kite-shape but the pure Muscular always tends toward a squareness of outline.

We repeat, he is no more "square" morally than any other type, so do not make the mistake of attributing any more of this virtue to him than to others.

¶ Each type has its own weaknesses and points of strength as differentiated from other types and these are responsible for most of the moral differences between people.

No Type Superior Morally

¶ Since moral weakness comes from type weakness and since each type possesses about as many weaknesses as the others, it follows that no type is superior "morally" to any other and no type is morally inferior to any other.

Type and Temptation

¶ Morality is mostly a matter of how much temptation you can withstand.

Every individual in a civilized community is surrounded by temptations of some kind most of the time. He does not want to yield to any of them. Every man and woman does the best of which his particular type is capable under a given circumstance.

Each individual resists many temptations for which we fail to give him credit. He yields only to those which make such a strong appeal to his type that he lacks the power of resistance.

In other words, each person yields to the temptations that prey upon his particular weaknesses, and what his weaknesses are will depend upon his type. In the grip of these temptations he may commit anything from discourtesy to crime—according to the strength of the temptation plus his own leaning in that direction.

On the other hand, certain "immoralities" which appeal strongly to some types have no attraction whatever for others and these latter get credit for a virtuousness that has cost them nothing.

Praise and Punishment

¶ On the other hand, each one of the five human types has certain points of strength and from these gets its natural "moral" qualities. We spend a great deal of energy giving praise and blame but when we realize—as we are doing more and more—that the type of an individual is responsible for most of his acts, we will give less of both to the individual and more of both to the Creator.

Type vs. Training

¶ The most that training can do is to brace up the weak spots in us; to cultivate the strong ones; to teach us to avoid inimical environments; and to constantly remind us of the penalties we pay whenever we digress.

Child Training

¶ As this great science of Human Analysis becomes known the world will understand for the first time "how the other half lives," and *why* it lives that way.

We will know why one child just naturally tells fibs while his twin brother, under identical training, just naturally tells the truth. What is more to the point we will know this in their childhood and be prepared to give to each the kind of training which will weed out his worst and bring out his best.

Short and Stocky

¶ The extreme Muscular type (See Chart 5) is below medium height, though one of any height may be largely muscular.

The extreme type, of which we are treating in this chapter, is shorter and heavier than the average. But his heaviness is due to *muscle* instead of fat. He has the appearance of standing firmly, solidly upon the ground, of being stalwart and strong.

The Square-Shouldered Man

¶ The Muscular's shoulders stand out more nearly at right angles than those of any other type and are much broader in proportion to his height. The Alimentive has sloping shoulders and the Thoracic inclines to high shoulders. But the shoulders of the pure Muscular are straighter and have a squareness where the Alimentive's have curves. This accounts for the fact that most of the square shouldered men you have known were not tall men, but medium or below medium in height. The wide square shoulders do not accompany any other pure type, though naturally they may be present in an individual who is a combination.

Has Proportionately Long Arms

¶ The arms of pure Musculars are longer in proportion to the body than the arms of other types. The arms of the Alimentive are short for his body but the extreme Muscular's arms are always anywhere from slightly longer to very much longer than his height would lead you to expect.

The Pure Muscular Head

¶ A "square head" is the first thing you think of when you look at a pure Muscular. His head has no such decided digressions from the normal as the round head of the Alimentive or the kite-shaped head of the Thoracic. It is not high for his body like the Thoracic's nor small for his body like the Alimentive's, but is of average proportions.

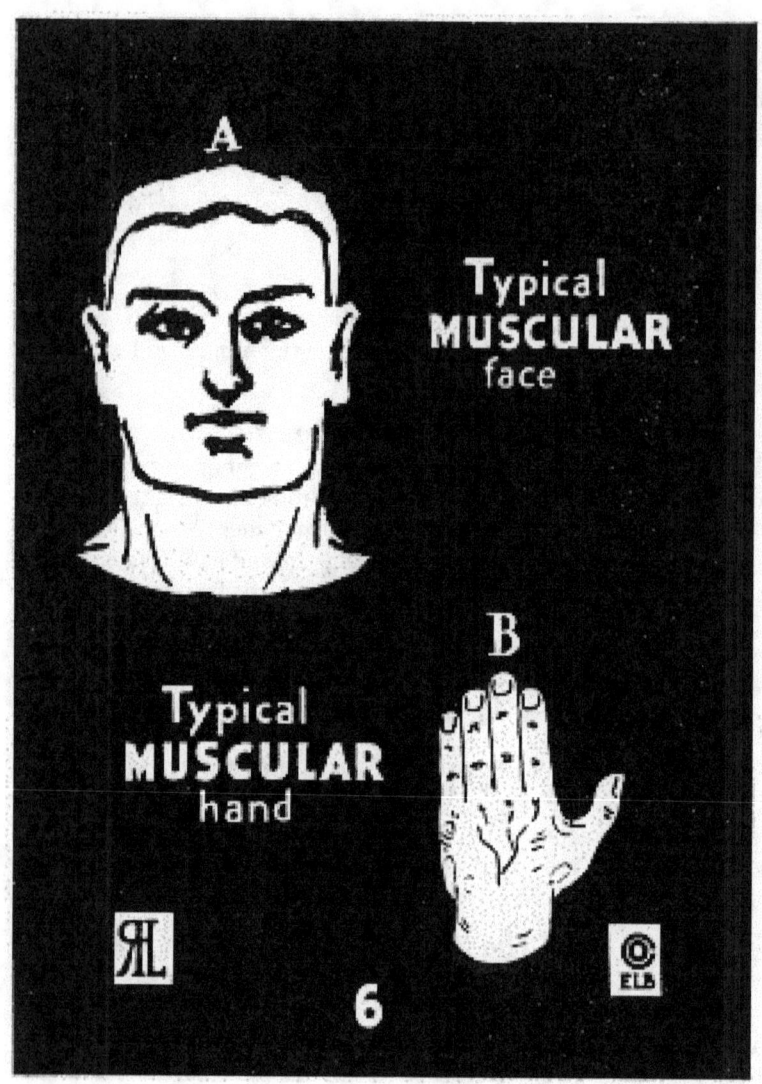

A

Typical
MUSCULAR
face

Typical
MUSCULAR
hand

B

6

His Thick Neck

¶ A distinctive feature of this type is his thick neck. It is not fat like that of the Alimentive nor medium long like that of the Thoracic but has unusual muscularity and strength.

This is one of the chief indications of the Muscular's strength. A sturdy neck is one of the most significant indications of physical prowess and longevity, while the frail neck—of which we shall speak in connection with the fifth type—is always a sign of the physical frailty which endangers life. The thickness of his neck may sometimes give you the impression that the

Muscular head is small but if you will look again you will see that it is normal for his bodily size.

His Square Face

¶ Looking at him from directly in front you will see that the Muscular's face gives you an impression of squareness. (See Chart 6) You will also notice that his side-head, cheeks and jaw run up and down in such a way as to give him a right-angled face.

His Square Jaw

¶ A broad jaw is another characteristic of this type. Not only is it square, looked at from the front, but you are pretty sure to note that the jaw bones, as they proceed downward under the ear, tend to make a right-angled turn at the corners instead of a rounded curve.

These dimensions tend to give the whole lower part of the Muscular's face a box-like appearance. It is considered becoming to men but robs its female owners of the delicate, pointed chin so much desired by women.

The Typical Muscular Hand

¶ Notice the hands of the people you meet and you will be surprised to see how different and how interesting they are. Their size, shape and structure as seen from the back of the hand are especially significant and tell us much more about the individual's nature than the palm does.

Perhaps you have thought that a hand was just a hand. But there are hands and hands. Each pure type has its own and no other is ever seen on the extreme of that type.

The hand of the Muscular, like all the rest of his body, is built in a series of squares. It runs out from the wrist and down in a straighter line and tends to right angles. (See Chart 6)

The Square Fingers of This Type

¶ "Spatulate fingers"—meaning fingers that are square or paddle-shaped at the tips—are sure indications of a decided muscular tendency.

He may have other types in combination but if his fingers are really square— "sawed off at the ends" in such a way as to give them large instead of tapering ends—that person has more than average muscularity and the activities of his life will tend in the directions referred to in this chapter.

The Manual Worker

¶ Musculars are the hand-workers of the world. They are the artisans, craftsmen, the constructors and builders.

We all tend to use most those organs or parts of the body which are largest and most highly developed. The Muscular's hand is proportionately larger than the hand of any other type. It has more muscle, that one element without which good hand work is impossible.

So it has followed inevitably that the manual work of the world is done largely by Musculars. Their hands are also so much more powerful that they do not tire easily.

The Hand of the Creative Artist

¶ "The artist's hand" and "the artistic hand" are phrases long used but misused. Delicate tapering fingers were supposed in ancient times to denote artistic ability. The frail curving hand was also supposed to be a sign of artistic talent.

From the stage of old down to the movies of today the typical artist is pictured with a slight, slender hand.

This tapering-fingered hand denotes a keen sense of artistic values; a love of the esthetic, refined and beautiful; and real artistic *appreciation*, but *not* the ability to create.

The "Hand Arts"

¶ Before we explain this, kindly understand that we are speaking only of those arts which require hand work—and not of such arts as singing, dancing, or musical composition which could more properly be called artistic activities. We are referring only to those arts which depend for their creation upon the human hand—such as painting, architecture, craftsmanship, cartooning, sculpture, violin, piano, etc.

All these are created by square fingered people.

We are too much inclined to think of the products of these arts as being created out of sheer artistic sense, artistic taste or artistic insight. But a moment's reflection will show that every tangible artistic creation is the result of unusual hand work combined with gifted head work. Without a sure, strong, well-knit hand the ideas of the greatest artists could never have materialized. The lack of such a hand explains why the esthetic, the artistic-minded and the connoisseur do not *create* the beautiful things they *appreciate*.

Head and Hand Partners

¶ The hand must execute what the brain plans and it must be so perfect a mechanism for this that it responds to the most elusive inspirations of the artist. It must be a fifty per cent partner, else its owner will never produce real art.

No type has this strong, sure, co-ordinated hand-machine to any such degree as the Muscular.

The finger ends, which are of the utmost significance in the creation of artistic things, must be fitted with well developed muscles of extreme efficiency or the execution will fall short of the ideal pictured in the artist's mind.

The pure Muscular type seldom makes an artist, for, after all, inspired brain work is the other important element in the creation of art, and this is the forte of the fifth type. A combination of the fifth type with the Muscular makes most

70

hand artists. A combination of the Muscular and Thoracic makes most singers. Every hand artist will be found to have spatulate-fingered hands—in short, muscular hands.

The hand of the famous craftsman, pianist, sculptor and painter, instead of being more frail and delicate, is always larger and heavier than that of the average person. Such a hand is a certain indication of the muscular element in that individual's makeup.

His Powerful Movements

¶ Forceful, decisive movements also characterize this type. He is inclined to go at even the most trivial things with as much force as if the world depended on it.

Recently we were exhibiting a small pencil sharpener to a muscular friend. It was so sharp that it performed its work without pressure. But she took hold of it as if it were a piece of artillery and pushed the pencil into it with all the force she had.

When we remonstrated smilingly—for her face and hands are ultra-square—she said, "But I can't do anything lightly. I just naturally put that much force into everything."

His Forceful Walk

¶ Heavy, powerful, forceful strides distinguish the walk of this type. If he has but ten steps to go he will start off as if beginning an around-the-world marathon.

You Hear Him Coming

¶ All Musculars notify people, by their walk, of their approach. They are unconscious of this loud incisive tread, and most of them will be surprised to read it here. But their friends will recognize it. The chances are that they have often spoken of it amongst themselves.

The Loud Voice

¶ The "steam-calliope voice" belongs almost always to a Muscular. He does his talking just as he does everything else—with all his might.

It is very difficult for the Muscular to "tone down" this powerful voice. His long-suffering friends will testify to this characteristic.

His Stentorian Tones

¶ This loud voice is a serious social handicap to him. His only chance of compensation for it lies in its use before juries, congregations or large audiences.

It might be noted here that every great orator has been largely of this type, and also that his fame came not alone from the things he said but from the stentorian tones in which he said them.

Famous Male Singers

¶ Caruso, John McCormack and all other famous male singers had large thoracic systems, but in every instance it was combined with a large muscular development.

The Solid Sitter

¶ When a Muscular sits down he does it as he does everything—with definiteness and force. He does not spill over as does the Alimentive nor drape himself gracefully like the Thoracic, but planks himself as though he meant business.

Activity His Keynote

¶ Because he is especially built for it the Muscular is more active than any other type. Without muscles no organism could move itself from the spot in which it was born.

Biology teaches us that the stomach was the first thing evolved. The original one-call organism possessed but one function—digestion. As life progressed it became necessary to send nutriment to those parts of the organism not touched by the stomach.

For the purpose of reaching these suburbs there was involved the circulatory or Thoracic system, and this gave rise, as we have seen in the previous chapter, to the Thoracic type.

Movement and Development

¶ As time went on movement became necessary, full development not being possible to any static organism. To meet this need muscles were evolved, and organic life began to move.

It was only a wiggle at first, but that wiggle has grown till today it includes every kind of labor, globe trotting and immigration.

The Muscular is fitted with the best traveling equipment of any type and invariably lives a life whose main reactions express these things.

The Immigrant Muscular

¶ No matter what his work or play the Muscular will make more moves during the course of a day than other types. He loves action because his muscles, being over-equipped for it, keep urging him from within to do things.

As a result this type makes up most of the immigrants of the world. Italians, Poles, Greeks, Russians, Germans and Jews are largely of this type and these are the races furnishing the largest number of foreigners in America.

Inertness Irks Him

¶ Shut up a Muscular and you destroy him. His big muscle system cries out for something to do. He becomes restless, nervous and ill when confined or compelled to be idle.

The Alimentive loves an easy time but the Muscular dislikes ease except when exhausted. Even then it is almost impossible to stop him.

Must Be Doing Something

¶ "I can't bear to be doing nothing!" you often hear people say. Such a person always has plenty of muscle. Musculars want to feel that they are not wasting time. They must be "up and doing," accomplishing something. If there is nothing near them that needs doing they are sure to go and find something.

The Born Worker

¶ Work is second nature to this type. He really prefers it.

Everyone likes some kind of work when in the mood if it serves a purpose or an ideal. But the Muscular likes work for its own sake—or rather for the activity's sake.

Work palls on the Alimentive and monotony on the Thoracic, but leisure is what palls on the Muscular. He may have worked ten years without a vacation and he may imagine he wants a long one, but by the morning of the third day you will notice he has found a piece of work for himself. It may be nothing more than hanging the screen door, chopping the wood or dusting the furniture, but it will furnish him with some kind of activity.

Because he enjoys action for its own sake and because work is only applied action, this type makes the best worker. He can be trusted to work harder than any other type.

Require Less Watching

¶ It is no accident that the three-hundred-men gangs of foreign workmen who dig ditches, tunnels and tubes, construct buildings, railroads and cities work with fewer foremen and supervisors than are ordinarily required to keep much smaller forces of other employees at their posts.

Seldom Unemployed

¶ For this reason the Muscular is seldom out of work. He is in demand at the best current wages because he can be depended upon to "keep at it."

¶ While writing this book our windows overlook a public park in one of America's one-million-population cities. Hundreds of unemployed men sleep there day and night. Having occasion to pass through this park daily for several months it has been interesting to note the types predominating. Hardly one per cent belonged to the Muscular type.

Likes To Do Things

¶ Because he is such a hard worker this type gets a good deal of praise and glory just as the fat people, who manage to get out of work, receive a good deal of blame. Yet work is almost as pleasant to the Muscular as leisure is to the Alimentive.

The Muscular's Pugnacity

¶ Fighters—those who really enjoy a scrap occasionally—are invariably Musculars. Their square jaws—the sure sign of great muscularity—are famous the world over and especially so in these days when war is once more in fashion.

The next time you look at the front faces of Pershing, Haig, Hindenberg or even that of your traffic policeman, note the extremely muscular face and jaw. Combat or personal fighting is a matter of muscle-action. Being well equipped for it this type actually enjoys it. That is why he is oftener in trouble than any other type.

It was no accident that the phrase "big stick" was the slogan of an almost pure Muscular.

Loves the Strenuous Life

¶ "The strenuous life" was another of Roosevelt's pet phrases and came from the natural leanings of his type. The true Muscular is naturally strenuous. Because we are prone to advise others to do what we enjoy doing ourselves it was inevitable that so strenuous a man as T. R. should advocate wholesale, universal and almost compulsory strenuosity.

We tell others to do certain things because "it will do you good" but the real reason usually is that we like to do it ourselves.

The Acrobatic Type

¶ The next time you go to a vaudeville show get there in time for the acrobatics and notice how all the participants are Musculars. If there are any other types taking part please observe that they are secondary to the acrobats—they catch the handkerchiefs or otherwise act as foils for the real performers.

All the hard work in the act will be done by Musculars. You will find no better examples of the short, stocky, well-knit pure Muscular than here. You do not need to wait for another show to realize how true this is. Recall the form and height of all the acrobats you have ever seen. You will remember that there was not one who did not fit the description of the pure Muscular given at the beginning of this chapter.

Acrobats Always Muscular

¶ We once had occasion to refer to this fact in a Human Analysis Class. One member declared that just that week he had seen a very tall, unmuscular man performing in an acrobatic act at the Orpheum.

Knowing that this was impossible, we offered a large reward to this member if he were proven right. We sent to the theater and found the acrobat in question. He had just finished his act and kindly consented to come over.

He turned out to be a pure Muscular as we had stated. The class member's mistake came from the fact that the acrobat appeared taller than he really was. High platforms always give this illusion. Furthermore his partner in the act was of diminutive height and the acrobat looked tall and slender by contrast.

Why They Don't Do It

¶ To be an acrobat is the ambition of almost every boy. There have been few who did not dream, while doing those stunts in the haymow on Mother's broomstick, of the glory that should be theirs when they grew up and performed in red tights for the multitudes.

Almost every boy has this ambition because he passes through a stage of decided muscular development in his early years. But only those who were born with much larger muscles than the average ever carry out their dreams. The others soon develop girth or the "sitting still" habit to the point where a cushioned seat in the first row of the parquet looks much better.

Durability in Clothes

¶ Something that will wear well is what this type asks for when he drops in to buy a suit. Musculars are not parsimonious nor stingy. Their buying the most durable in everything is not so much to save money as for the purpose of having something they do not need to be afraid to handle.

Likes Heavy Materials

¶ This type likes heavy, stable materials. Whereas the Alimentive wants comfortable clothes and the Thoracic distinctive ones the Muscular wants wearable, "everyday" clothes.

He wants the materials to be of the best but he cares less for color than the Thoracic. Quality rather than style and plainness rather than prettiness are his standards in dress.

"Making over father's pants for Johnnie" is a job Muscular women have excelled in and for which they have become famous. For this type of mother not only sees to it that father's pants are of the kind of stuff that won't wear out easily but she has the square, creative hand that enjoys construction.

The Plain Dresser

¶ Simple dresses—blue serge, for instance—are the ones the Muscular woman likes. This type cares little about clothes as ornamentation. He is intent on getting his desires satisfied by DOING things, not by looking them. He also resents the time and trouble that fashionable dressing demands. No matter how much money this type has he will not be inclined to extremes in dress. Musculars are not really interested in clothes for clothes' sake. It is not that this type is unambitious. He is extremely so, but he is so concentrated on "getting things done" that he is likely to forget how he looks while doing them.

When a person of this type does take great pains with his clothes it is always for a purpose, and not because he enjoys preening himself. There is little of the peacock in the Muscular.

A Simple Soul

¶ Musculars are the most democratic of all the types. The Thoracic is a natural aristocrat, and enjoys the feeling of a little innocent superiority. But Musculars often refuse to take advantage of superior positions gained through wealth or station, and are inclined to treat everybody as an equal. It is almost impossible for this type, even though he may have become or have been born a millionaire, to "lord it over" servants or subordinates. He is given to backing democratic movements of all kinds. This explains why Musculars constitute the large majority in every radical group.

Humanness His Hobby

¶ Being "human" is an ideal to which this type adheres with almost religious zeal. He likes the commonplace things and is never a follower after "the thing" though he has no prejudices against it, as the fourth type has.

An Everyday Individual

¶ The Muscular does not care for "show" and, except when essential to the success of his aims, seldom does anything for "appearances."

He is not an easy-going companion like the Alimentive nor a scintillating one like the Thoracic, but an everyday sort of person.

When in Trouble

¶ This type is not given to sliding out of difficulties like the Alimentive nor to being temporarily submerged by them like the Thoracic. He "stands up to them" and backs them down. When in trouble he acts, instead of merely thinking.

The Most Practical Type

¶ "The Practicalist" is often used to describe this type. He is inclined to look at everything from the standpoint of its practicality and is neither stingy nor extravagant.

He Likes What Works

¶ "Will it work?" is the question this type puts to everything. If it won't, though it be the most fascinating or the most diverting thing in the world, he will take little interest in it.

This type depends mostly upon his own hands and head to make his fortune for him, and is seldom lured into risking money on things he has not seen.

The Natural Efficiency Expert

¶ The shortest, surest way is the one this type likes. He is not inclined to fussiness. He insists on things being done in the most efficient way and he usually does them that way himself. He is not an easy man to work for, but quick to reward merit. The Muscular does not necessarily demand money nor the things that money buys but he tries to get the workable out of life.

The Property Owner

¶ This type likes to have a fair bank account and to give his children a worth while training. He is less inclined to bedeck them with frills but he will plan years ahead for their education.

These are not rigid parents like the fourth type, lenient like the Alimentives, nor temperamental with their children like the Thoracics, but practical and very efficient in their parenthood. They are very fond of their children but do not "spoil" them as often as some of the other types do.

They bring up their children to work and teach them early in life how to do things. As a result, the children of this type become useful at an early age and usually know how to earn a living if necessary.

Wants the Necessities

¶ The necessities of life are things this type demands and gets. Whereas the Alimentive demands the comforts and the Thoracic the unusual, the Muscular demands the essentials. He is willing to work for them, so he usually succeeds.

He is not given to rating frills and fripperies as necessities but demands the things everyday men or women need for everyday existence. Naturally he goes after them with the same force he displays in everything else.

His Heart and Soul in Things

¶ When some one shows great intensity of action directed toward a definite end we often say "he puts his heart and soul into it." This phrase is apropos of almost everything the Muscular does. He makes no half-hearted attempts.

An Enthusiast

¶ "Enthusiasm does all things" said Emerson, and therein explained why this type accomplishes so much. The reason back of the Muscular's enthusiasm is interesting.

All emotions powerfully affect muscles. A sad thought flits through your mind and instantly the muscles of your face droop and the corners of your mouth go down. Hundreds of similar illustrations with which you are already familiar serve to prove how close is the connection between emotions and muscles. The heart itself is nothing more nor less than a large, tough, leather-like muscle.

Possessing the best equipment for expressing emotion, the Muscular is constantly and automatically using it.

Therefore he becomes an enthusiast over many things during the course of his lifetime. This enthusiasm literally burns his way to the things he wants.

The Plain Talker

¶ When deeply moved this type talks well. If the mental element is also strong he can become a good public speaker for he will then have all the qualifications—a powerful voice, human sympathy, democracy and simplicity.

In private conversation he is inclined to use the verbal hammers too much and to be too drastic in his statements, accusations, etc. But he means what he tells you, no more, and usually not much less.

He avoids long words and complicated phrases even when well educated and speaks with directness and decisiveness.

Straightforward

¶ "Straight from the shoulder" might be used to describe the method of the pure Muscular in what he does and says. He does not deal in furbelows, dislikes the superfluous and the superficial. He goes through life over the shortest roads.

Likes the Common People

¶ Plain folks like himself are the kind this type prefers for friends. He enjoys them immensely, but does not cultivate as large a number of them as does the Thoracic, nor have as many "bowing acquaintances" as the Alimentive.

Snubs the Snobs

¶ The snob is disliked by every one but is the especial aversion of this type. Being so democratic himself and living his life along such commonplace lines, he has no patience with people who imagine they are better than others or who carry the air of superiority.

The only person therefore whom the Muscular is inclined to snub is the snob. He is not overawed by him and enjoys "taking him down a peg," whenever he tries his high and mighty airs on him.

Defends the "Under Dog"

¶ Standing by the under dog is a kind of religion with this type. He glories in fighting for the downtrodden. This explains why he is so often a radical. Much of this vehemence in radicalism is due to the fact that he feels he is getting even with the snobs of the world—the plutocrats—when he furthers the causes of the proletariat.

Often on the Warpath

¶ To "have it out" with you is the first inclination of this type when he becomes angry.

He is apt to say atrocious things and to exaggerate his grievances. Everything must yield to his "dander" once it is up. Being possessed of a highly developed fighting equipment, he is like a battleship, with every gun in place, most of the time.

He is frequently in violent quarrels with his friends, and since he does not recover from his anger quickly like the Thoracic, he often loses them for life.

The Most Generous Friend

¶ When they like you the Musculars are the most abandoned in their generosity of all the types. They "go the limit" for you, as the Westerner says, and they go it with their money, time, love and enthusiasm.

All types do this for short periods occasionally and for a very few choice friends. But the Muscular often does it for people he scarcely knows if they strike his fancy or appeal to him.

His heart and his home belong to the stranger almost as completely as to his family, for he does not feel a stranger to any one. He feels from the first moment, and acts, as though he had known you always.

This accounts for his democracy, for his success as an orator, and—sometimes for his being "broke."

Not a Quick Forgiver

¶ But disappoint him in anything he considers vital and he does not overlook it easily. He finds it especially difficult to forgive people who take advantage of the generosity he so lavishly extends. But he does not make his hate a life-long one, as the fourth type does.

With all his own giving to others he seldom takes much from others.

The Naturally Independent

¶ "Standing on his own legs" is a well-known trait of the Muscular. Dependence is bred of necessity. This type being able to get for himself most of the things he wants, rarely finds it necessary to call upon others for assistance.

Love of self-government, plus fighting pluck, both of which are inherent in the Muscular Irish race, are responsible for the long struggle for their independence.

Likes Plain Foods

¶ "Meat and potatoes" are the favorite diet of the average American Muscular. The Alimentive wants richness and sweetness in food, the Thoracic wants variety and daintiness but the Muscular wants large quantities of plain food.

The Alimentive specializes in desserts, the Thoracic in unusual dishes, but the Muscular wants solid fare. He is so fond of meat it is practically impossible for him to confine himself to a vegetable diet.

When He is in Moderate Circumstances

¶ The Muscular is most often found in moderate circumstances. He is rarely far below or far above them. Most of the plain, simple, everyday things he desires can be secured by people of average means. He does not feel the necessity for becoming a millionaire to obtain comforts like the Alimentive, nor for extravagances like the Thoracic.

When He is Rich

¶ Philanthropy marks the expenditures of this type whenever he is rich. He does not spend as much of his money for possessions but enjoys investing it in what he deems the real—that is, other human beings.

The most plain and durable things in furnishings, architecture and service characterize the rich of this type in their homes.

The World's Work Done by Musculars

¶ Broadly speaking, the fat man manages the world, the florid man entertains the world, and the muscular man does the work of the world.

He composes most of the day-laborers, the middle men, the manual and mechanical toilers the world around, as we have stated before.

He could get out of his hard places into better paid ones if he did not like activity so well, but lacking the love of ease and show he is willing to work hard for the necessities of life.

Simple Habits

¶ The Muscular's nature does not demand the exciting, the gregarious or the food-and-drink things that lead toward laxity.

He is seldom a dissipator. He likes to go to bed early, work hard and make practical progress in his life.

He leads the simple and yet the most strenuous existence of any type.

Entertainment He Enjoys

¶ Plays about plain people, their everyday experiences, hopes and fears are the kind that interest this type most.

The "problem play" of a decade ago was a prime favorite with him. He likes everything dealing with these everyday commonplace affairs with which he is most familiar.

He frequently goes to serious lectures—something the pure Alimentive always avoids—and he especially enjoys them if they deal with the problem of the here and now.

He cares little for comic opera, vaudeville or revues because he feels they serve no practical purpose and get him nowhere. This type does not attend the theater merely to be amused. He goes for light on his everyday experiences and usually considers time wasted that is spent solely on entertainment.

Music He Likes

¶ Band music, stirring tunes and all music with "go" to it appeals to this type.

Reading

¶ True stories, news and the sport page are the favorite newspaper reading of the Muscular. He does not take to sentimental stories so much as the Alimentive, nor to adventure so much as the Thoracic but sticks to practical subjects almost exclusively.

Being active most of his waking hours, and strenuously active at that, the Muscular is often too tired at night to read anything.

His Favorite Sports

¶ The most violent sports are popular with this type. Football, baseball, handball, tennis, rowing and pugilism are his preferences. All experts in these lines are largely Muscular.

Physical Assets

¶ His wonderful muscular development, upon which depends so much of life's happiness—since accomplishment is measured so largely thereby—is the greatest physical asset of this type. With it he can accomplish almost anything of which his mind can conceive.

He is capable of endless effort, does not tire easily, and because of his directness makes his work count to the utmost of his mental capacity.

Physical Liabilities

¶ A tendency to overwork is the chief physical pitfall of this type. The disease to which he is most susceptible is rheumatism. But owing to his love of activity he exercises more than any other type and thus forestalls many diseases.

Social Assets

¶ His generosity is the strongest social asset of the Muscular. He is usually straightforward and sincere and thereby gains the confidence of those who meet him.

Social Liabilities

¶ His loud voice and his plain ways are the disadvantages under which this type labors in social intercourse. He needs polishing and is not inclined to take it. His pugnacity is also a severe drawback.

Emotional Assets

¶ Understanding, enthusiasm and warmth of heart are the emotional qualities which help to make him the public leader he so often is. These have made him the "born orator," the radical and the reformer of all ages.

Emotional Liabilities

¶ His tendency to anger and combat are shackles that seriously handicap him. Many times these lose him the big opportunities which his splendid traits might obtain for him.

Business Assets

¶ Efficiency and willingness to work hard and long are the greatest business assets of this type.

Business Liabilities

¶ Pugnacity over trifles costs the average Muscular many business chances. He has to fight out every issue and while he is doing it the other fellow closes the deal.

He is inclined to argue at great length. This helps him as a lawyer or speaker but it hurts him in business. Curbing his combativeness in business should be one of his chief aims.

Domestic Strength

¶ Practical protection for the future is the greatest gift of the average Muscular to his family. He is not as lenient with his children as is the Alimentive nor as effusive as the Thoracic, but he usually lays by something for their future.

Domestic Weakness

¶ Cruel, angry words do the Muscular much harm in his family life. They cause his nearest and dearest to hold against him the resentments that follow.

Should Aim At

¶ Taking more frequent vacations, relaxing each day, and curbing his pugnacity should be the special aims of this type.

Should Avoid

¶ Superficial and quarrelsome people, all situations requiring pretence, and everything that confines and restricts his physical activity should be avoided by this type.

Strongest Points

¶ Democracy, industry and great physical strength are the strongest points of this type.

Weakest Points

¶ Inclination to overwork and to fight constitute the Muscular's two weakest links.

How to Deal with this Type Socially

¶ Don't put on airs nor expect him to when you are meeting this type socially. Be straightforward and genuine with him if you would win him.

How to Deal with this Type in Business

¶ Remember, this type is inclined to be efficient and democratic and you had better be the same if you wish to succeed with him in business.

He is intensely resentful of the man who tries to put anything over on him; and demands efficiency. So when you promise him a thing see to it that you deliver the goods and for the price stated. He does not mind paying a good price if he knows it in the beginning, but beware of raising it afterwards. The Muscular is serious in business, not a jollier like the Alimentive, nor a thriller like the Thoracic, and he wants you to be the same.

Remember, the chief distinguishing marks of the Muscular, in the order of their importance, are LARGE, FIRM MUSCLES, A SQUARE JAW and SQUARE HANDS. Any person who has these is largely of the Muscular type, no matter what other types may be included in his makeup.

CHAPTER IV

The Osseous Type

"The Stayer"

en and women in whom the Osseous or bony framework of the body is more highly developed than any other system are called the Osseous type.

This system consists of the bones of the body and makes what we call the skeleton.

Just as the previous systems were developed during man's biological evolution for purposes serving the needs of the organism—first, a stomach-sack, then a freight system in the form of arteries to carry the food to remoter parts of the body, and later muscles with which to move itself about—so this bony scaffolding was developed to hold the body upright and better enable it to defend and assert itself.

Man is a creature who, in spite of his height, walks erect. He can so do only by means of the support given him by his bony framework. The human body is like a tall building—the muscles are like the mortar and plaster, the bones are like the steel framework around which everything else is built and without which the structure could not stand upright.

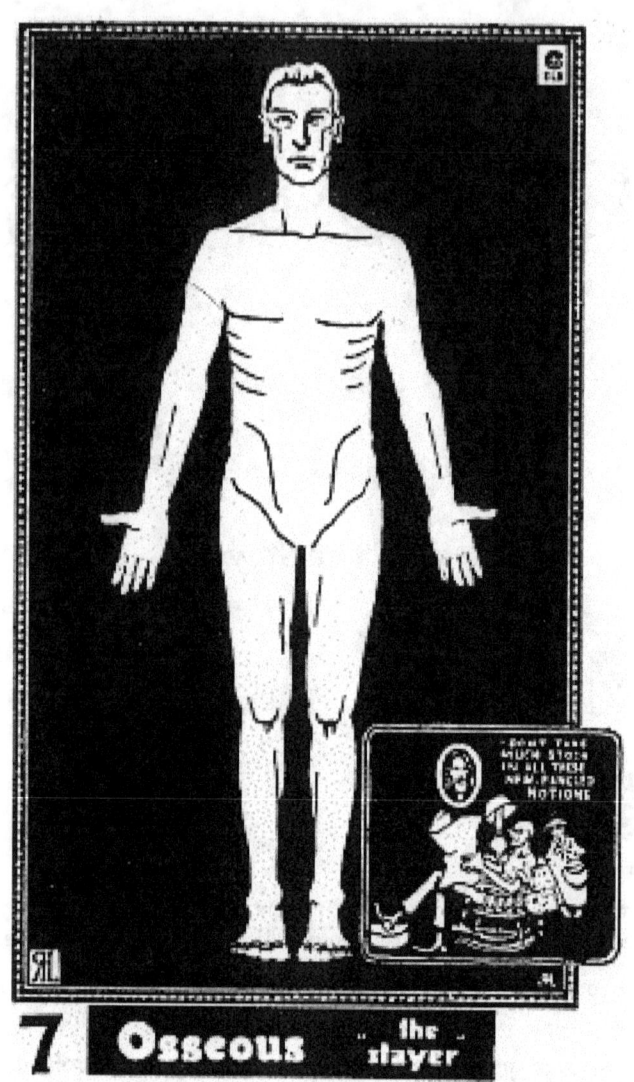

7 Osseous "the slayer"

How to Know Him

¶ Prominent ankles, wrists, knuckles and elbows are sure signs that such an individual has a large osseous or bony element in his makeup.

When you look at any person you quickly discern whether fat, bone or muscle predominates in his construction. If fat predominates he leans toward the Alimentive, no matter what other types he may have in combination; if firm, well-defined muscles are conspicuous, he is largely Muscular; but if his bones are *proportionately large for his body* he has much of the Osseous type in his makeup.

The "Raw-Boned" Man

¶ "Raw-boned" exactly describes the appearance of the extreme Osseous. (See Chart 7)

Such a man is a contrast to others in any group and a figure with which all of us are familiar. But that his inner nature differs as widely from others as his external appearance differs from theirs is something only recently discovered.

As we proceed through this chapter you will be interested to note how every trait attributed to this type applies with absolute accuracy to every extremely raw-boned, angular person you have ever known. You will also notice how these traits have predominated in every person whose bones were large for his body.

Though this type was the last to be classified by science it is the most extreme of them all.

Physical Rigidity

¶ An impression of physical rigidity is given by the extreme Osseous. Such a man or woman looks stable, unchanging, immovable—as though he could take a stand and keep to it through thick and thin.

So vividly do very tall, angular, raw-boned people convey this impression that they are seldom approached by beggars, barked at by street vendors, or told to "step lively."

His Size Looks Formidable

¶ The power of his physique is evident to all who look at him. The strength indicated by his large joints, angular hands and general bulk intuitively warns others to let this kind of person alone.

He is therefore unmolested for the most part, whether he walks down the streets of his home town or wanders the byways of dangerous vicinities.

His Ruggedness

¶ This type also looks rugged. He reminds us of "the rugged Rockies." He appears firm, fixed, impassive—as though everything about him was permanent.

Externals are not accidental; they always correspond to the internal nature in every form of life. And it is not accidental that the Osseous looks all of these things. He is all of them as definitely as they can be expressed in human nature.

The Steady Man

¶ Of all human types the Osseous is the most dependable and reliable. The phrases, "that man is steady," "never flies off the handle," "always the same," etc., are invariably used concerning those of more than average bony structure.

Immovability His Keynote

¶ The keynote of the bony man's whole nature—mental, physical and moral—is immovability.

Once he settles into a place of any kind—a town, a home, or even a chair—he is disinclined to move. He does not settle as quickly as other types but when he does it is for a longer stay.

Think how different he is from others in this psychological trait and how it coincides exactly with his physiological structure.

The fat man lets you make temporary dents in his plans just as you make them in a piece of fat meat. But the bony man is exactly the opposite, just as bone is difficult to twist, or turn, or alter in any way. It takes a long time and much effort—but once it is changed it is there for good.

The "Six-Footer"

¶ Because any individual's height is determined by his skeleton, extreme tallness is a sign of a larger than average bony structure. The extreme Osseous is therefore tall.

But you must remember that large joints are more significant than height. Even when found in short people they indicate a large osseous tendency.

Large Bones for His Body

¶ So bear in mind that any person whose *bones are large for his body* is somewhat of the Osseous type, regardless of whether he is short or tall and regardless of how much fat or muscle he may have. The large-jointed person when fat is an Osseous-Alimentive. A large-jointed man of muscle would be an Osseous-Muscular.

The "Small Osseous"

¶ A very short person then may be predominantly Osseous if his bones are proportionately large for his body. Such an individual is called a "Small Osseous."

A head that is high for his body and inclines to be straight up and down goes with the extreme Osseous type. (See Chart 8) It does not resemble a sphere like the Alimentive, is not kite-shaped like the Thoracic, nor square like the Muscular. It is higher than any of the others, stands on a longer, more angular neck, and his "Adam's Apple" is usually in evidence.

The Pioneer Type

¶ Like each of the other types, the Osseous is a result of a certain environment. Rigorous, remote regions require just such people, and these finally gave rise to this stoical nature. The outposts of civilization are responsible for his evolution.

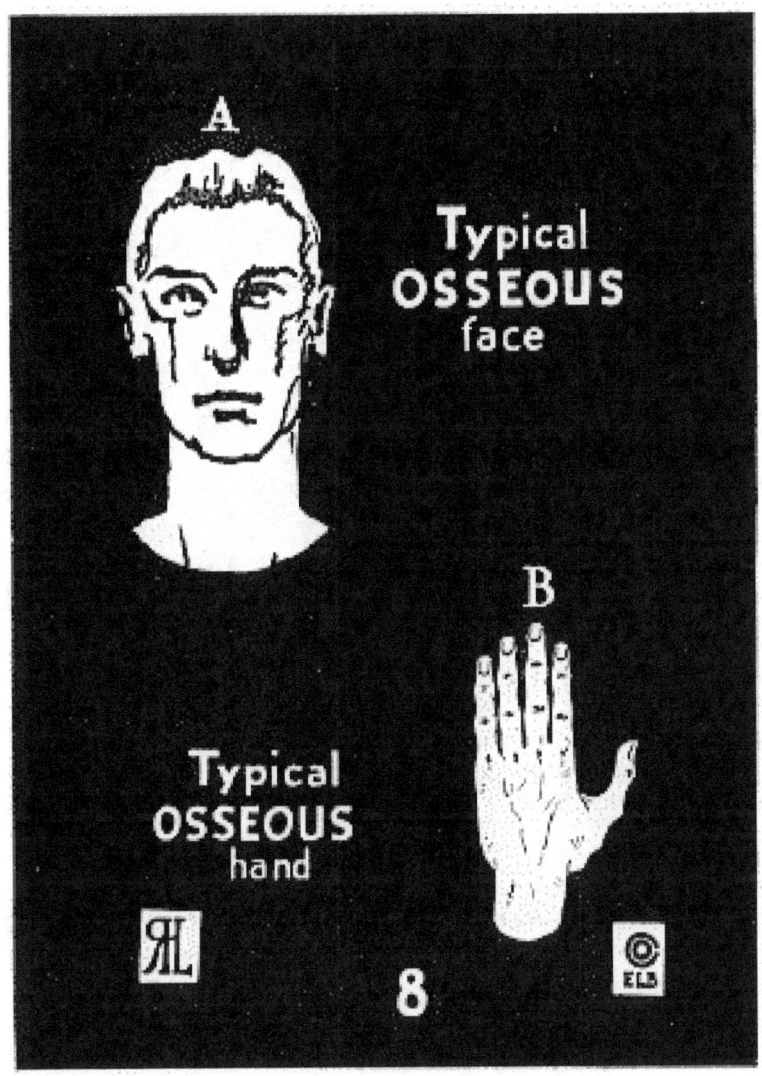

Typical **OSSEOUS** face

Typical **OSSEOUS** hand

8

Pioneering, with its hardship, its menacing cold and dearth of comforts, in far countries at last produced a man who could stand them, who could "live through" almost anything and still dominate his surroundings.

Not a "Softie"

¶ The Osseous does not give way to his feelings. He keeps his griefs, sorrows, ambitions and most of his real opinions to himself. He is the farthest from a "softie" of any type.

If you desire to know at once what kind of person the Osseous is, put the Alimentive and Thoracic types together and mix them thoroughly. The Osseous is the *opposite* of that mixture.

Each and every trait he possesses is one whose exact opposite you will find in one or the other of these first two types.

Consistency in Types

¶ As we go on in this chapter you will see why all kinds of people make up the world, for Nature has outdone herself in the distinctions between the five human types.

Each type is made up of certain groups of traits with which we have come in contact all our lives but which we have never classified; and each "set" of traits comprising a type has a consistency which nothing less than Mother Nature could have produced. You will be interested to see how accurate are the statements concerning each type and how they are proven again and again in every type you associate with.

Guesswork is no longer necessary in the sizing up of strangers. You can know them better than their mothers know them if you will get these nutshells of facts clearly in your mind and then *apply* them.

His High Cheek Bones

¶ Cheek bones standing higher than the average are always indicative either of a large Thoracic or a large Osseous element.

If the distance between the cheeks is so wide as to make this the widest section of the face, it is probable that the person is more Thoracic than Osseous. But if his face is narrow across the cheek bones, and especially if it runs perpendicularly down to the jaw-corners from that point instead of tapering, the person is large of the Osseous type.

Built on the Oblong

¶ An oblong is what the Osseous brings to mind. His body outlines approximate the oblong—a squareness plus length. He is full of right angles and sharp corners. (See Chart 7)

His face is built on the oblong (See Chart 8) and if you will notice the side-head of the next Osseous man you meet you will see that even a side view presents more nearly the appearance of the oblong than of any other geometrical figure.

The Oblong Hand

¶ "The gnarled hand" well describes that of the Osseous. The hand outlines of this type also approximate the oblong. (See Chart 8) It runs straight down instead of tapering when the fingers are held close together.

The hand of the Osseous matches his body, head and face. It is bony, angular, large-jointed and as rigid as it looks. The inflexibility of his hand is always apparent in his handshake.

Knotty Fingers

¶ Knotty fingers characterize the hands of this type. Their irregular appearance comes from the size of the joints which are large, in keeping with all the joints running throughout his organism.

Everything in one of Nature's creatures matches the other parts. Agassiz, the great naturalist, when given the scale of a fish could reconstruct for you the complete organism of the type of fish from which it came. Give a tree-leaf to a botanist and he will reconstruct the size, shape, structure and color of the tree back of it. He will describe to you its native environment and its functions; what its bark, blossoms and branches look like and what to do to make it grow.

No Guesswork in Nature

¶ Nature has no accidents. With her everything is organized, everything has a purpose, and every part of a thing, inside and out, matches the whole. So the hand of the Osseous and the face of the Osseous match the body and head.

This is also true of every other type. The Alimentive has small, fat, dimpled hands and feet like his body; the Thoracic has tapering hands and feet to match his face and body; the Muscular's body, hands and feet are all square; but the Osseous has a bony body, so his hands and feet are equally bony.

The Man of Slow Movements

¶ "He is too slow for me," you have heard some one say of another. Perhaps you heard it said today. Review the outward appearance of all the people you know who have this reputation, from those of your earliest childhood down to that person of whom it was spoken today—and you will find that every one of them resembled the bony type we have just been describing.

Look back and call to mind the appearance of all the "rapid" ones and you will find that in every case they possessed high color, high chests or high-bridged noses. Take another look for the easy-going amenable ones, and see how plump they all were!

The Straight-Laced

¶ None of these things "just happened." They are the result of the law of cause and effect. The connection between external and internal traits is becoming clearer every day and reveals some very unexpected things.

One that has been discovered very recently is that the straight-faced are the straight-laced. Notice for yourself and you will find that every person who is really "straight-laced" is a person with a straight face—that is, a face with straighter up-and-down lines than the average.

Think back over those you have known who come under this heading and you will find no actually round-faced people amongst them.

No matter how sanctimonious, religious or correct a person may act when his position or the occasion demands it, if he has a round, "moon" face he is not really straight-laced at heart. Any one who knows him well enough to know his real nature will tell you so.

The Naturally Conventional

¶ The "born Puritan," the ascetic, and the naturally conventional person is, on the other hand, invariably an individual of more severe facial outlines.

This person may be in an unconventional position; your straight-faced, severe-lined person may be a gambler, a boot-legger, or follow any other line defying the conventions; but he is at heart a conservative after all. For instance, you will always find, when you know him, that he does things in a way that is very conventional to him. That is, he has decided standards, rules, habits and requirements, and he clings rigidly to them in the transaction of his business, regardless of how lax the business itself may be.

"A certain way of doing things" means as much to him, at heart, as it means little to the circular-faced people.

Systematic and Methodical

¶ "A place for everything and everything in its place" is a rule preached and practised by people of this type.

The Osseous person does not mislay his things. He knows so well where they are that he can "go straight to them in the dark." Such a man is careful of his tools and keeps his work-bench or desk "shipshape." A woman of this type is an excellent housekeeper. Her sewing basket, dresser drawers and pantry shelves are all systematically arranged in apple-pie order.

The typical New England housewife, who washes on Mondays, irons on Tuesdays and bakes on Saturdays for forty years, is a direct descendant of the Puritans, most of whom belong to this bony, pioneering type.

The Stiff Sitter

¶ Extremely Osseous people are inclined to be somewhat formal in their movements. They make fewer motions than any other type. They do not wave their hands or arms about when talking and are almost devoid of gesticulation of any kind. They sit upright instead of slumping down in their chairs, except when tall and lanky, and usually prefer "straight-backs" to rockers.

The Osseous Walk

¶ The extremely raw-boned person has also a formal gait. His walk, like all his other movements, is inclined to be deliberate and somewhat mechanical.

¶ Nothing about the five types is more interesting than the walk which distinguishes each. The Alimentive undulates or rolls along; the Thoracic is an impulsive walker, and the Muscular is forceful in his walk. But the Osseous walks mechanically, deliberately, and refuses to hurry or speed up.

The Naturally Poised

¶ The Osseous has more natural poise than any other type.

He is not impressionable, excitable or arousable. Things do not "stir him up" as they do other people. He is more self-contained, self-controlled and self-sufficient than any other. He is not easily carried off his feet and seldom yields to impulse. It is difficult to get him to do anything on the spur of the moment. He usually has his evenings, Sundays and vacations all planned in advance and won't change his schedule.

Not Given to "Nerves"

¶ Literally as well as figuratively the Osseous is not a man of "nerves." Every fiber of his being is less susceptible to outside stimuli than that of other types. In this he is the exact opposite of the Thoracic whose nerves, as we have pointed out, are so finely organized that he is hypersensitive.

Resists Change

¶ Osseous people do not change anything, from their hair dress to their minds, any oftener than necessary. When they do, it is for what they consider overpoweringly good reasons.

These people are not flighty. They have their work, their time and their lives laid out systematically and do not allow trivialities to upset them. They take a longer time to deliberate on a proposed line of action, but once they have made a decision, adhere to it with much greater tenacity than any other type.

The Constant

¶ People of this type are not fickle nor flirtatious. They love few; but once having become enamored are not easily turned aside. It is this type that remains true to one love through many years, sometimes for life.

The Implacable

¶ The Osseous are not prone to sudden outbursts of temper. But they have the unbending kind when it is aroused.

Never forgiving and never forgetting is a trait of these people as contrasted with the Thoracic.

The Alimentive avoids those he does not like and forgets them because it is too much bother to hate; the Thoracic flames up one moment and forgives the next; the Muscular takes it out in a fight then and there, or argues with you about it.

But the Osseous despises, hates and loathes—and keeps on for years after every one else has forgotten all about it. The "rock-bound Puritan" type, as stony as the New England land from which it gets its living, is always bony. The implacable father who turns his child away from home, with orders "never to darken his door again," always has a lot of bone in his structure. Those who refuse to be softened into forgiveness by the years are always of this type.

Not Adaptable

¶ It is difficult for the Osseous to "fit in." He is not adaptable and in this is once again the opposite of the Thoracic. It is impossible for him to adjust himself quickly to people or places.

Because he is unyielding, unbending and unadjustable he is called "sot in his ways."

He should not be misjudged for this inadaptability, however, for it is as natural to him as smoothness is to the Alimentive and impulsiveness to the Thoracic. He is made that way and is no more to blame for it than you are for having brown eyes instead of blue.

The One-Track Man

¶ "Single-track minds" are characteristic of this type. They get an idea or an attitude and it is there to stay. They think the same things for many years and follow a few definite lines of action most of their lives.

But it is to be remembered in this connection that this type often accomplishes more through his intensive concentration than more versatile types. While they follow many by-paths in search of their goal the Osseous sticks to the main track.

The Born Specialist

¶ "This one thing I do," is a motto of the Osseous. They are the least versatile of any type and do not like to jump from one kind of work to another.

They prefer to do one thing at a time, do it well and finish it before starting anything else. Because of this the Osseous stars in specialities.

Dislikes Many Irons in the Fire

¶ The man who likes many irons in the fire is never an Osseous. To have more than one problem before him at one time makes him irritable, upset and exasperated.

The Most Dependable Type

¶ The unchangingness which handicaps the Osseous in so many ways is responsible for one very admirable trait. That trait is dependability.

The Osseous is reliable. He can be taken at his word more often than any other type, for he lives up to it with greater care.

Always on Time

¶ When an Osseous person says, "I will meet you at four o'clock at the corner of Main and Market," he will arrive at Main and Market at *four* o'clock. He will not come straggling along, nor plead interruptions, nor give excuses. He will be on the exact spot at the exact hour.

In this he is again a contrast to the first two types. An Alimentive man will roll into the offing at a quarter, or more likely, a half hour past the time, smilingly apologize and be so naive you forgive and let it go at that.

The Thoracic will arrive anywhere from five after four to six o'clock, drown you in a thrilling narrative of just how it all happened, and never give you a chance to voice your anger till he has smoothed it all out of you.

An Exacting Man

¶ But the Osseous is disdainful of such tactics and you had better beware of using them on him. He is dependable himself and demands it of others—a little trait all of us have regarding our own particular virtues.

Likes Responsibility

¶ Responsibility, if it does not entail too many different kinds of thought and work, is enjoyed by the Osseous.

He can be given a task, a job, a position and he will attend to it. Entrust him with a commission of any kind, from getting you a certain kind of thread to discovering the North Pole, and he will come pretty near carrying it out, if he undertakes it.

Finishes What He Starts

If an Osseous decides to do a piece of work for you you can go ahead and forget all about it. No need to advise, urge, watch, inspire, coax and cajole him to keep him at it. He prefers to keep at a thing if he starts it himself. You may have to hurry him but you will not have to watch him in order to know he is sticking to his task. This type starts few things but he brings those few to a pretty successful conclusion.

The Martyr of the Ages

¶ "Died for a cause" has been said of many people, but those people have in every known instance been possessed of a larger-than-average bony structure.

¶ The pure Alimentive seldom troubles his head about causes. The Thoracic is the type that lives chiefly for the pleasure of the moment and the adventures of life. The Muscular fights hard and works hard for various movements.

But it is the Osseous who dies for his beliefs.

It is the Osseous or one who is largely of this type who languishes in prison through long years, refusing to retract.

He is enabled to do this because the ostracism, jibes and criticism with which other types are finally cowed, have little effect upon him. On the contrary, opposition of any kind whets his determination and makes him keep on harder than ever.

Takes the Opposite Side

¶ "If you want him to do a thing, tell him to do the opposite," is a well-known rule supposed to work with certain kinds of people.

You have wondered why it sometimes worked and sometimes didn't, but it is no mystery to the student of Human Analysis.

When it worked, the person you tried it on was an Osseous or one largely osseous in type; and when it didn't he was of some other type.

"Contrary?" complained a man of a bony neighbor recently, "Contrary is his middle name."

"I am open to conviction but I would like to see the man who could convince me!" is always said by a man whose type you will be sure to recognize.

An "Againster"

¶ "I don't know what it is but I'm against it," is the inside mental attitude of the extremely raw-boned, angular man or woman.

They often, unconsciously, refrain from making a decision about a thing till the other fellow makes his. That settles it; they take the other side.

Think back over your school-days and call to mind the visage and bodily shape of the boy who was always on the opposite side, who just naturally disagreed, who "stood out" against the others. He was a bony lad every time.

Remember the "Fatty" with a face like a full moon? Did he do such things? He did not. He was amenable, easy-going, good natured, and didn't care how the discussion came out, so long as it didn't delay the lunch hour.

Remember the boy or girl who had the pick of the school for company whenever there was a party, who danced well and was so sparkling that you always felt like a pebble competing against a diamond when they were around? That boy or girl had a high chest, or high color, or a high-bridged nose—and usually all three.

But the one you couldn't persuade, who couldn't be won over, who refused to give in, who held up all the unanimous votes till everybody was disgusted with him, and who rather gloried in the distinction—that boy had big bones and a square jaw—the proof that he was a combination of the Osseous and Muscular types.

The Human Balance Wheel

¶ To keep the rest of the world from running away with itself, to prevent precipitous changes in laws, customs and traditions, has always been one of the functions performed for society by the bony people.

These people are seldom over-persuaded, and being able to retain a perpendicular position while the rest of the world is being swayed this way and that, they act as society's balance wheel.

The Osseous changes after a while, but it is a long while, and by the time he does, the rest of the world has marched on to something new which he opposes in its turn.

Wears Same Style Ten Years

¶ Even the clothes worn by this type tell the same story. Styles may come and styles may go, but the Osseous goes on forever wearing the same lines and the same general fashions he wore ten years before. If you will recall the men who continued wearing loose, roomy suits long after the "skin-tight" fashions came in, or the women who kept to long, full skirts when short ones were the vogue you will note that every one of them had large joints or long faces.

Bony people find a kind of collar or hat that just suits, and to that hat and that collar they will stick for twenty years!

Disdains the Fashions

¶ In every city, neighborhood and country crossroads there is always somebody who defies the styles of today by wearing the styles of ten years ago.

Every such person is a bony individual—never under any circumstances a moon-faced, round-bodied one. In every case you will find that his face is longer, his nose is longer, or his jaw and hands are longer than the average—all Osseous indications.

When He is Rich

¶ The bony man's adherence to one style or to one garment is not primarily because he wishes to save money, though saving money is an item that he never overlooks. It is due rather to his inability to change anything about himself in accordance with outside influence until a long time has elapsed.

Doesn't Spend Money Lavishly

¶ The Osseous is, as stated at the head of this chapter, a "stayer" and this applies to everything he wears, thinks, says, believes, and to the way he carries on every activity of his life.

No matter how rich he may be he will not buy one kind of car today and another tomorrow, nor one house this week and another in six weeks.

He uses his money, as all of us do, to maintain his type-habits and to give freer rein to them, not to change them to any extent. This type likes sameness. He likes to "get acquainted" with a thing. He never takes up fads and is the most conservative of all types. Unlike the Thoracic, he avoids extremes in everything and dislikes anything savoring of the "showy" or conspicuous.

Not a Social Star

¶ Because he dislikes display, refuses to yield to the new fangled fashions of polite society and finds it hard to adapt himself to people, the man of this type is seldom a social success.

He is the least of a "ladies' man" of all the types. The Osseous woman is even less disposed to social life than the Osseous man because the business and professional demands, which compel men of this type to mingle with their fellows, are less urgent with her.

Likes the Same Food

¶ The same "yesterday, today and forever" is the kind of food preferred by this type. He seldom orders anything new. The tried and true things he has eaten for twenty-five years are his favorites and it is almost impossible to win him away from them. "I have had bread and milk for supper every Sunday night for thirty years," a bony man said to us not long ago.

Means What He Says

¶ The Osseous does not flatter and seldom praises. Even when he would like to, the words do not come easily. But when he does give you a compliment you may know he means it. He is incisive and specific—a little too much so to grace modern social intercourse where so much is froth.

A Man of Few Words

¶ A man of few words is always and invariably a man whose bones are large for his body. The fat man uses up a great many pleasant, suave, merry, harmless words; the Thoracic inundates you with conversation; the Muscular argues, declares and states; but the Osseous alone is sparing of his words.

The Hoarder

¶ Bony people are never lavish with anything. They do not waste anything nor throw anything away. These are the people who save things and store them away for years against the day when they may find some use for them. When they do part with them it is always to pass them on "where they will do some one some good."

Careful of Money

¶ You never saw a stingy fat man in your life. Imagine a two-hundred-pound miser! Neither have you ever seen a really stingy man who was red-faced and high-chested. Nor have you ever found a real Muscular who was a "tightwad."

But you have known some people who were pretty close with their money. And every one of them was inclined to boniness.

When He is Poor

¶ Bony men are seldom "broke" for they are more careful of expenditures than any other type. Even when they receive small salaries this type of person always has something laid by. But the extreme Osseous never makes a million. The same caution which prevents his spending much money also prevents the plunges that make big money.

¶ The Osseous cares more for money than any one else. This is what has enabled him, when combined with some other type, to be so successful in banking—a business where you risk the other man's money, not your own.

The extreme Osseous is never lax or extravagant with his money no matter how much he has. He never believes in paying any more for a thing than is necessary. Take note of the men who carry purses for silver instead of letting their change lie loose in their pockets. They are bony every time! Fat people and florid people are the ones who let their greenbacks fall on the floor while paying the cashier!

Fear of the Future

¶ "The rainy day" doesn't worry the fat people or the florid ones, but it is seldom out of the consciousness of the bony men and women. So they cling to their twenty-dollar-a-week clerkships for years because they are afraid to tackle anything entailing risk.

Pays His Bills

¶ "I had rather trust a bony man than any other kind," is what the credit experts have told us. "Other things being equal, he is the most reliable type in money matters, and pays his bills more promptly."

¶ The bony man is one who seldom approaches the credit man, however. He usually has enough to get the few things he really wants and if not he waits till he has.

Extremely bony husbands give their wives smaller allowances in proportion to their total income than any other type, and because they are systematic themselves they are more likely to ask for reports and itemizations as to where it goes.

The fat husbands and the florid husbands are the ones who give their wives their last cent and never ask what becomes of it.

The Repressed Man

¶ The Osseous man or woman is always somewhat repressed. Unlike the Thoracic, who uncorks and bubbles like a champagne bottle, he keeps the lid on his feelings.

Bony people are always more reticent than others. They invariably tell less of their private or personal affairs. One may live across the hall from a bony man for years without knowing much about him. He is as secretive as the Thoracic is confiding and as guarded as the Alimentive is naive.

Loyal to His Few Friends

¶ "Once your friend always your friend" can be said about the Osseous oftener than any other type.

¶ The Osseous does not make friends easily and is not a "mixer" but keeps his friends for many years. He "takes to" very few people but is exceedingly loyal to those of his choice.

The "Salt of the Earth"

¶ People of the Osseous type say little, they do little for you and they do not gush—but they are always there when you need them and "always the same." They write few letters to you when away, and use few words and little paper when they do. They are likely to fill every page, to write neatly, to waste no margins and to avoid flourishes. Their letters seldom require an extra stamp.

Plans Ahead

Foresight, laying plans far into the future, and keeping an eye out for breakers ahead, financially and otherwise, are tendencies which come natural to the Osseous.

He does not like to wait until the last moment to do a thing. He dislikes unexpectedness and emergencies of any kind. He is always prepared. For instance a bony person will think out every move of a long journey before boarding his train. Weeks in advance he will have the schedule marked and put away in his coat pocket—and he knows just which coat he is going to wear too!

The Longest Lived

¶ The Osseous lives longer than any other type, for two reasons. The first is that his lack of "nerves" saves him from running down his batteries. He seldom becomes excited and does not exhaust himself in emotional orgies.

The second is that he habitually under-eats—usually because he does not care so much for food as the first three types, but quite often because he prefers to save the money.

People He Dislikes

¶ The bony man does not like people who try to speed him up, hurry him, or make him change his habits. Flashy people irritate him. But his worst aversions are the people who try to dictate to him. This type can not be driven. The only way to handle him is to let him think he is having his own way.

Likes the Submissive

¶ Amenable people who never interfere with him yet lend themselves to his plans, desires and eccentricities are the favorites of this type.

Diseases He is Most Susceptible To

¶ No diseases can be said to strike the Osseous more frequently than any other type.

But moodiness, fear—especially financial fear—long-sustained hatreds and resentments, and lack of change are indirectly responsible for those diseases which bring about the end, in the majority of cases.

Music He Likes

¶ Martial, classical music and ballads are favorites with the Osseous. Old-time tunes and songs appeal to him strongly.

Jazz, which the Alimentive loves, is disliked by most bony people.

Reading He Prefers

¶ Only a few kinds of reading, a few favorite subjects and a few favorite authors are indulged in by this type.

He will read as long as twenty-five years on one subject, master it and ignore practically everything else. When he becomes enamored of an author he reads everything he writes.

Reading that points directly to some particular thing he is really interested in makes up many of his books and magazines.

He is the kind of man who reads the same newspaper for half a century.

Physical Assets

¶ His great endurance, capacity for withstanding hardship, indifference to weather, and his sane, under-eating habits are the chief physical assets of this type.

Physical Liabilities

¶ This type has no physical characteristics which can be called liabilities except the tendency to chronic diseases. Even in this he runs true to form— slow to acquire and slow to cure.

His Favorite Sports

¶ Hiking and golf are the favorite sports of this type because these demand no sudden spurts of energy. He likes them because they can be carried on with deliberation and independence. He does not care for any sport involving team work or quick responses to other players. Except when combined with the Thoracic type he especially avoids tennis.

Favorite Entertainments

¶ Serious plays in which his favorite actors appear are the entertainments preferred by this type. He cares least of all for vaudeville.

Social Assets

¶ The Osseous has no traits which can properly be called social assets. His general uprightness comes nearest to standing him in good stead socially, however.

Social Liabilities

¶ Stiffness, reticence, physical awkwardness and the inability to pose or to praise are the chief social handicaps of this type.

Emotional Assets

¶ The Osseous is not emotional and can not be said to possess any assets that are purely emotional.

Emotional Liabilities

¶ The lack of emotional fervor and enthusiasm prevents this type from impressing others.

Business Assets

¶ Keeping his word, orderliness and system are the chief business assets of this type.

Business Liabilities

¶ A disinclination to mix, the inability to adapt himself to his patrons and a tendency to hold people too rigidly to account are the business handicaps of the Osseous.

Domestic Strength

¶ Constancy and faithfulness are his chief domestic assets.

Domestic Weaknesses

¶ Tightness with money, a tendency to be too exacting and dictatorial, and to fail to show affection are the things that frequently prevent marriage for the Osseous and endanger it when he does marry.

Should Aim At

¶ The Osseous should aim at being more adjustable to people and to his environment in general. He should try to take a greater interest in others and then *show* it.

Should Avoid

¶ Indifference and the display of it, solitude and too few interests are things the Osseous needs to avoid.

His Strong Points

¶ Dependability, honesty, economy, faithfulness and his capacity for finishing what he starts are the strongest points of this type.

His Weakest Points

¶ Stubbornness, obstinacy, slowness, over-cautiousness, coldness and a tendency to stinginess are the weakest links in people of the extreme Osseous type.

How to Deal with this Type Socially

¶ There is little to be done with the Osseous when you meet him socially except to let him do what he wants to do.

Don't interfere with him if you want him to like you.

How to Deal with this Type in Business

¶ As an employee, give him responsibility and then let him alone to do it his way.

Then keep your hands off.

Don't give him constant advice; don't try to drive him.

Let him be as systematic as he likes.

When dealing with him in other business ways rely on him and let him know you admire his dependability.

Remember, the distinguishing marks of the Osseous, in the order of their importance, are PROPORTION ATELY LARGE BONES FOR THE BODY, PROMINENT JOINTS and A LONG FACE. Any person who has these is largely of the Osseous type no matter what other types may be included in his makeup.

CHAPTER V

The Cerebral Type

"The Thinker"

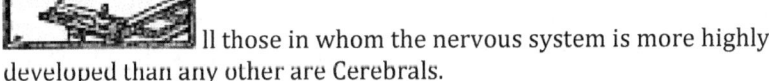

ll those in whom the nervous system is more highly developed than any other are Cerebrals.

This system consists of the brain and nerves. The name comes from the cerebrum or thinking part of the brain.

Meditation, imagining, dreaming, visualizing and all voluntary mental processes take place in the cerebrum, or brain, as we shall hereinafter call it. The brain is the headquarters of the nervous system—its "home office"—just as the stomach is the home office of the Alimentive system and the heart and lungs the home office of the Thoracic.

Your Freight System

¶ The Thoracic system may be compared to a great freight system, with each of its tributaries—from the main trunk arteries down to the tiniest blood vessels—starting from the heart and carrying its cargo of blood to every part of the body by means of the power furnished by the lungs.

Your Telegraph System

¶ But the nervous system is more like an intricate telegraph system. Its network of nerves runs from every outlying point of the body into the great headquarters of the brain, carrying sense messages notifying us of everything heard, seen, touched, tasted or smelled.

As soon as the brain receives a message from any of the five senses it decides what to do about it and if action is decided on, sends its orders back over the nerve wires to the muscles telling them what action to perform.

Your Working Agents

¶ This latter fact—that the muscles are the working agents of the body—also explains why the Muscular type is naturally more active than any of the others.

Source of Your Raw Materials

¶ The body may be compared to a perfectly organized transportation system and factory combined. The Alimentive system furnishes the raw materials for all the systems to work on.

Stationary Equipment

¶ The bones of the body are like the telegraph poles, the bridges and structures for the protection and permanence of the work carried on by the other systems of the body.

Now poles, bridges and structures are less movable, less alterable than any of the other parts of a transportation system, and likewise the bony element in man makes him less alterable in every other way than he would otherwise be. A predominance of it in any individual indicates a preponderance of this immovable tendency in his nature.

Mind and matter are so inseparably bound up together in man's organism that it is impossible to say just where mind ends and matter begins. But this we know: that even the mind of the bony person partakes of the same unbending qualities that are found in the bones of his body.

"Every Cell Thinks"

¶ Thomas A. Edison, as level-headed and unmystical a scientist as lives, says, "Every cell in us thinks." Human Analysis proves to us that something very near this is the case for it shows how the habitual mental processes of every individual are always "off the same piece of goods" as his body.

Thus the fat man's mind acts as his body acts—evenly, unhurriedly, easefully and comfortably. The florid man's mind has the same quickness and resourcefulness that distinguish all his bodily processes. The muscular man's mind acts in the same strenuous way that his body acts, while the bony man's brain always has an immovable quality closely akin to the boniness of his body.

He is not necessarily a "bonehead," but this phrase, like "fathead," is no accident.

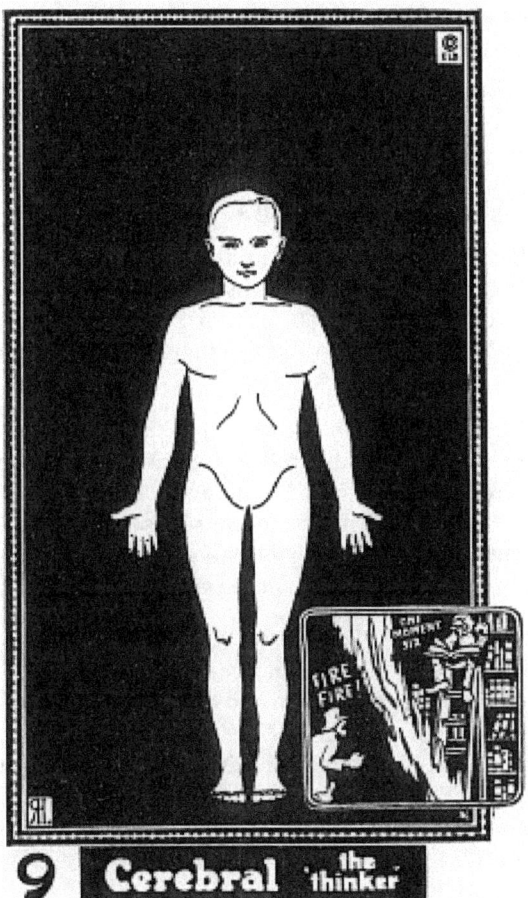

9 **Cerebral** the thinker

The Large Head on the Small Body

¶ As pointed out before, the larger any organ or system the more will it tend to express itself. So, the large-headed, small-bodied man runs more to mental than to physical activities, and is invariably more mature in his thinking. (See Chart 9) Conversely, the Alimentive type gets its traits from that elemental stage in human development when we did little but get and assimilate food, and when thinking was of the simplest form. In those days man was more physical than mental; he had a large stomach but a small head.

So today we see in the pure Alimentive type people who resemble their Alimentive ancestors. They have the same proportionately large stomach and proportionately small head,—with the stomach-system dominating their thoughts, actions and lives.

The Cerebral is the exact opposite of this. He has a top-heavy head, proportionately large for his body, and a proportionately undeveloped stomach system.

His Small Assimilative System

¶ The extreme Cerebral differs from other types chiefly in the fact that while his head is unusually large compared to the body, his alimentive, thoracic, muscular and bony systems are smaller and less developed than the average. The latter fact is due to the same law which causes the Alimentive to have a large body and a small head. Nature is a wonderful efficiency engineer. She provides only as much space as is required for the functioning of any particular organ, giving extra space only to those departments that need it.

The Cerebral-Alimentive is the combination which makes most of the "magnates" and the self-made millionaires. Such a man has all the Alimentive's desires for the luxurious comforts and "good things of life," combined with sufficient brains to enable him to make the money necessary to get them.

Nature doesn't give the pure Alimentive a large skull because he doesn't need it for the housing of his proportionately small brain, but concentrates on giving him a big stomach fitted with "all modern conveniences." On the other hand, the head of the Cerebral is large because his brain is large. The skull which is pliable and unfinished at birth grows to conform to the size and shape of the brain as the glove takes on the shape of the hand inside it.

Stomach vs. Brain

¶ Because the Alimentive and Cerebral systems are farthest removed from each other, evolutionally, a large brain and a large stomach are a very unusual combination. Such an individual would be a combination of the Alimentive and Cerebral types and would have the Alimentive's fat body with a large highbrow head of the Cerebral. The possession of these two highly developed but opposite kinds of systems places their owner constantly in the predicament of deciding between the big meal he wants and the small one he knows he should have for good brain work.

We are so constructed that brain and stomach—each of which demands an extra supply of blood when performing its work—can not function with maximum efficiency simultaneously.

Why Light Lunches

¶ When your stomach is busy digesting a big meal your brain takes a vacation. This little fact is responsible for millions of light luncheons daily. The strenuous manual worker can empty a full dinner pail and profit by it but the brain worker long ago discovered that a heavy midday meal gave him a heavy brain for hours afterwards.

Clear Thinking and a Clear Stomach

¶ Clear thinking demands a clear stomach because an empty stomach means that the blood reserves so necessary to vivid thinking are free to go to the brain. Without good blood coursing at a fairly rapid rate through the brain no man can think keenly or concentratedly. This explains why you think of so many important things when your stomach is empty that never occur to you when your energy is being monopolized by digestion.

Heavy Dinners and Heavy Speeches

¶ All public speakers have learned that a heavy dinner means a heavy speech.

Elbert Hubbard's rule when on his speaking tours was one every orator should follow. "Ten dollars extra if I have to eat," said Fra Elbertus—a far cry from the days when we "fed up" the preacher at Sunday dinner with the expectation of hearing a better sermon!

Uses His Head

¶ Just as assimilation is the favorite activity of the Alimentive type, head work is the favorite activity of the large-headed Cerebral. He is so far removed, evolutionally, from the stomach stage that his stomach is as much a remnant with him as the brain is a rudiment with the extreme Alimentive.

The extra blood supply which nature furnishes to any over-developed part of the body also tends to encourage him in thinking, just as the same condition encourages the fat man in eating.

Forgets to Eat

¶ An Alimentive never forgets dinner time.

But the Cerebral is so much more interested in food for his brain than food for his body that he can go without his meals and not mind it. He is likely to have a book and a cracker at his meals—and then forget to eat the cracker!

Physical Sensitivity

¶ We are "mental" in proportion to the sensitiveness of our mental organization. The Cerebral possesses the most highly developed brain center of any type and is therefore more sensitive to all those stimuli which act upon the mind.

His whole body bespeaks it. The fineness of his features is in direct contrast to some of the other types. The unusual size of his brain denotes a correspondingly intricate organization of nerves, for the nerves are tiny elongations of the brain.

The intellectual sensitiveness of any individual can be accurately estimated by noting the comparative size of his brain and body.

His Triangular Head and Face

¶ A triangle is the geometrical figure approximated by the Cerebral's front face and head.

If he is a pure, extreme Cerebral a triangle is again what you are reminded of when you look at his head from the side, for his head stands on a small neck, his forehead stands out at the top, while his back head is long. These bring the widest part of his head nearer the top than we find it in other types.

Delicate Hands

¶ A thin, delicate hand denotes a larger-than-average Cerebral element. (See Chart 10)

Smooth Fingers

¶ What have long been known as "smooth fingers" are typical of the Cerebral. These are not to be confused with the fat, pudgy babyish fingers of the Alimentive, for though the latter's fingers are smooth around, they do not present straight outlines at the sides. They puff out between the joints.

Smooth fingers are characteristic of the extreme Cerebral type. They are called this because their outlines run straight up and down.

The joints of the Alimentive finger (See Chart 2) mark the narrowest places owing to the fact that the joints are not changeable. In the Osseous fingers (See Chart 8) the opposite is true. The joints mark the widest spots and the spaces between are sunken.

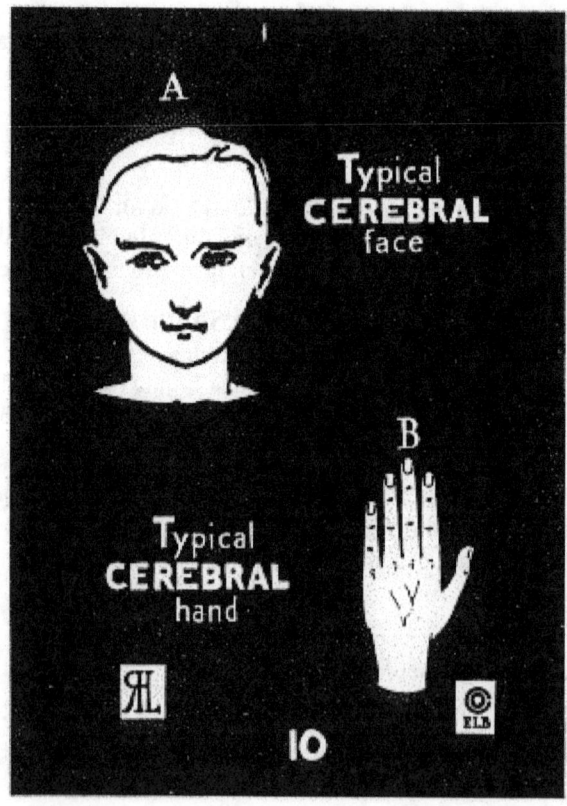

A
Typical
CEREBRAL
face

B

Typical
CEREBRAL
hand

10

The fingers of the Thoracic are inclined to be pointed like his head, while the Muscular's fingers are square at the end and look the power they possess.

¶ But the Cerebral has fingers unlike any of these. There is no fat to make them pudgy and no muscle to make them firm. Neither are there large joints to make them knotty. Their outlines therefore run in almost straight lines and the whole hand presents a more frail, aesthetic appearance.

Meditation His Keynote

¶ Thinking, contemplating, reflecting—all the mental processes coming under the head of "meditation"—constitute the keynote of this type.

The Alimentive lives to eat, the Thoracic to feel, the Muscular to act, the Osseous to stabilize, but the Cerebral lives to meditate.

Air Castles

¶ He loves to plan, imagine, dream day-dreams, visualize and go over and over in his mind the manifold possibilities, probabilities and potentialities of many things.

When he carries this to extremes—as the person with a huge head and tiny body is likely to do—he often overlooks the question of the practicability of the thing he is planning. He inclines to go "wild-catting," to dream dreams that are impossible of fruition.

Thought for Thought's Sake

¶ He will sit by the hour or by the day thinking out endless ultimates, for the sheer pleasure it gives him. Other men blame him, criticise him and ridicule him for this and for the most part he does fail of the practical success by which the efficient American measures everything.

But the fact must never be forgotten that the world owes its progress to the men who could see beyond their nose, who could conceive of things no one had ever actually seen.

This type, more than any other, has been the innovator in all forms of human progress.

The Dreamer

¶ "Everything accomplished starts with the dream of it," is a saying we all know to be true. Yet we go on forever giving all the big prizes to the doers. But the man who can only dream lives in a very hostile world. His real world is his thoughts but whenever he steps out of them into human society he feels a stranger and he is one.

Doesn't Fit

¶ The world of today is ruled by people who accomplish. "Putting it over," "delivering the goods," "getting it across," are a part of our language because they represent the standards of the average American today.

The Cerebral is as much out of place in such an environment as a fish is on dry land. He knows it and he shows it. He doesn't know what the other kind are driving at and they know so little of what he is driving at that they have invented a special name for him—the "nut."

Doing isn't his line. He prefers the pleasures of "thinking over" to all the "putting over" in the world. This type usually is a failure because he takes it all out in dreaming without ever doing the things necessary to make his dream come true.

A "Visionary"

¶ These predilections for overlooking the obvious, the tangible and the necessary elements in everyday existence tend to make of the Cerebral what he is so often called—a "visionary."

For instance, he will build up in his mind the most imposing superstructure for an invention and confidently tell you "it will make millions," but forget to inform himself on such essential questions as "will it work?" "Is it transportable?" or "Is there any demand for it?"

Ahead of His Time

¶ "He was born ahead of his time" applies oftenest to a man of this type.

He has brains to see what the world needs and not infrequently sees how the world could get it. But he is so averse to action himself that unless active people take up his schemes they seldom materialize.

What We Owe to the Dreamers

¶ Men in whom the Cerebral type predominated anticipated every step man has made in his political, social, individual, industrial, religious and economic evolution. They have seen it decades and sometimes centuries in advance. But they were always ridiculed at first.

The Mutterings of Morse

¶ History is replete with the stories of unappreciated genius. In Washington, D. C., you will have pointed out to you a great elm, made historic by Samuel Morse, inventor of the telegraph. He could not make the successful people of his day give him a hearing, but he was so wrapped up in his invention that he used to sit under this tree whenever the weather permitted, and explain all about it to the down-and-outers and any one else who would stop. "Listen to the mutterings of that poor old fool" said the wise ones as they hurried by on the other side of the street. But today people come from everywhere to see "The Famous Morse Elm" and do homage to the great mind that invented the telegraph.

"Langley's Folly"

¶ Today we fly from continent to continent and air travel is superseding land and water transportation whenever great speed is in demand. A man receives word that his child is dangerously ill; he steps into an airplane and in less than half the time it would take trains or motors to carry him, alights at his own door.

Commerce, industry, war and the future of whole nations are being revolutionized by this man-made miracle. Yet it is but a few short years since S. P. Langley was sneered at from one end of this country to the other because he stooped to the "folly" of inventing a "flying machine."

The Trivial Telephone

¶ Alexander Graham Bell invented the telephone. But it was many years before he could induce anybody to finance it, though some of the wealthiest, and therefore supposedly wisest, business men of the day were asked to do so. None of them would risk a dollar on it. Even after it had been tested at the Centennial Exposition in Philadelphia and found to work perfectly, its possibilities were so little realized that for a long while no one could be found to furnish the funds necessary to place it upon the market.

The Wizardry of Wireless

¶ Then after the world had become accustomed to transacting millions of dollars worth of business daily over the once despised telegraph and telephone it took out its doubts on Marconi and his "wireless telegraphy." "It's impossible," they said. "Talk without wires? Never!"

But now the radio needles pierce the blue from San Diego to Shanghai and from your steamer in mid-ocean you can say good night to your loved one in Denver.

Frank Bacon's Play

¶ Ideas always have to go begging at first, and the greater the idea the rougher the sledding.

The most successful play ever put on in America was "Lightnin'," written by Frank Bacon, a typical Cerebral-Osseous. It ran every night for three years in New York City. It has made a million people happy and a million dollars for its sponsors. But when Mr. Bacon, who also plays the title role, took it to the New York producers they refused it a try-out. But because he had faith in his dream and persisted, his name and his play have become immortal.

An Ideal Combination

¶ The ideal combination is a dreamer who can DO or a doer who knows the power of a DREAM. Thinking and acting—almost every individual is doing too much of one and too little of the other!

The World's Two Classes

¶ The world is divided roughly into these two classes: those who act without thinking (and as a result are often in jail); and those who think without acting (and as a result are often in the poorhouse).

To be a Success

¶ To be a successful individual today you have got to dream and then DO; plan and then PRODUCE; contemplate and then CONSTRUCT; think it out and then WORK it out.

If you do the latter at the expense of the former you are doomed to work forever for other people, to play some other man's game. If you do the former at the expense of the latter you are doomed to know only the fringes of life, never to be taken seriously and never to achieve.

Pitfalls for Dreamers

¶ If you are inclined to take your pleasure out in cerebrating instead of creating; if it suffices you to see a thing in your imagination whether it ever comes to pass or not, you are at a decided disadvantage in this hustling world; and you will never be a success.

Pitfalls for the Doer

¶ On the other hand if you are content to do what other men dream about and never have dreams of your own you will probably always have a berth but will never have a million. You will exist but you will never know what it is to live.

The Hungry Philosopher

¶ The extreme Cerebral can sit on a park bench with an empty purse and an empty stomach and get as much pleasure out of reflecting on the "whichness of the what and the whitherness of the wherefore" as an Alimentive gets out of a planked steak. Needless to say, each is an enigma to the other. Yet most people imagine that because both are human and both walk on their hind legs they are alike. They are no more alike than a cow and a canary.

His Frail Body

¶ The extreme Cerebral type finds it difficult to do things because, as we have seen, he is deficient in muscle—one of the vital elements upon which activity and accomplishment are based. This type has little muscle, little bone, and little fat.

Deficient in "Horse Power"

¶ He is not inactive for the same reason that the Alimentive is; his stomach processes do not slow him down. But his muscles are so undeveloped that he has little inward urge toward activity and little force back of his movements. His heart and lungs are small, so that he also lacks "steam" and "horse power."

He prefers to sit rather than to move, exactly as the Muscular prefers to be "up and doing" rather than to sit still.

The Man of Futile Movements

¶ Did you ever look on while a pure Cerebral man tried to move a kitchen stove? Ever ask the dreamer in your house to bring down a trunk from the attic?

Will you ever forget the almost human perversity with which that stove and that trunk resisted him; or how amusing it looked to see a grown man outwitted at every turn by an inert mass?

"I have carried on a life-long feud with inanimate things," a pure Cerebral friend remarked to us recently. "I have a fight on my hands every time I attempt to use a pair of scissors, a knife and fork, a hammer or a collar button."

His Jerky Walk

¶ Because he is short the Cerebral takes short steps. Because he lacks muscle he lacks a powerful stride. As a result he has a walk that is irregular and sometimes jerky.

When he walks slowly this jerk is not apparent, but when hurried it is quite noticeable.

Is Lost in Chairs

¶ The Cerebral gets lost in the same chair that is itself lost under the large, spreading Osseous; and for the same reason. Built for the average, chairs are as much too large for the Cerebral as they are too small for the big bony man. So the Cerebral's legs dangle and his arms don't reach.

Dislikes Social Life

¶ Though a most sympathetic friend, the Cerebral does not make many friends and does not care for many. He is too abstract to add to the gaiety of social gatherings, for these are based on the enjoyment of the concrete.

Enjoys the Intellectuals

¶ Readers, thinkers, writers—intellectuals like himself—are the kinds of people the Cerebral enjoys most.

Another reason why he has few friends is because these people, being in the great minority, are not easy to find.

Ignores the Ignorant

¶ People who let others do their thinking for them and those who are not aware of the great things going on in world movements, are not popular with this type. He sometimes has a secret contempt for them and ignores them as completely as they ignore him.

Avoids the Limelight

¶ Modesty and reserve, almost as marked in the men as in the women, characterize this extreme type. They do things of great moment sometimes—invent something or write something extraordinary—but even then they try to avoid being lionized.

They prefer the shadows rather than the spotlight. Thus they miss many of the good things less brainy and more aggressive people gain. But it does no good to explain this to a Cerebral. He enjoys retirement and is constantly missing opportunities because he refuses to "mix."

Cares Little for Money

¶ Friends mean something to the Cerebral, fame sometimes means much but money means little. In this he is the exact opposite of the Osseous, to whom the pecuniary advantages or disadvantages of a thing are always significant.

The pure Cerebral finds it difficult to interest himself in his finances. He seldom counts his change. He will go away from his room leaving every cent he owns lying on the dresser—and then forget to lock the door!

This type of person almost never asks for a raise. He is too busy dreaming dreams to plan what he will do in his old age. He prefers staying at the same job with congenial associates to finding another even if it paid more.

Very Often Poor

¶ Since we get only what we go after in this world, it follows that the Cerebral is often poor. To make money one must want money. Competition for it is so keen that only those who want it badly and work with efficiency ever get very much of it.

The Cerebral takes so little interest in money that he gets lost in the shuffle. Not until he wakes up some morning with the poorhouse staring him in the face does he give it serious consideration. And then he does not do much about it.

Almost Never Rich

¶ History shows that few people of the pure Cerebral type ever became rich. Even the most brilliant gave so much more thought to their mission than the practical ways and means that they were usually seriously handicapped for the funds necessary to its materialization.

Madame Curie, co-discoverer of radium, said to be the greatest living woman of this type, is world-famous and has done humanity a noble service. But her experiments were always carried on against great disadvantages because she had not the financial means to purchase more than the most limited quantities of the precious substance.

About Clothes

¶ Clothes are almost the last thing the Cerebral thinks about. As we have seen, all the other types have decided preferences as to their clothes—the Alimentive demands comfort, the Thoracic style, the Muscular durability and the Osseous sameness—but the extreme Cerebral type says "anything will do." So we often see him with a coat of one color, trousers of another and a hat of another, with no gloves at all and his tie missing.

Often Absent-Minded

¶ We have always said people were "absent-minded" when their minds were absent from what they were doing. This often applies to the Cerebral for he is capable of greater concentration than other types; also he is so frequently compelled to do things in which he has no interest that his mind naturally wanders to the things he cares about.

A Cerebral professor whom we know sometimes appeared before his Harvard classes in bedroom slippers. A Thoracic would not be likely to let his own brother catch him in his!

Writes Better than He Talks

¶ The poor talker sometimes surprises us by being a good writer. Such a one is usually of the Cerebral type.

He likes to think out every phase of a thing and put it into just the right words before giving it to the world. So, many a Cerebral who does little talking outside his intimate circle does a good deal of surreptitious writing. It may be only the keeping of a diary, jotting down memoranda or writing long letters to his friends, but he will write something. Some of the world's greatest ideas have come to light first in the forgotten manuscripts of people of this type who died without showing their writings to any one. Evidently they did not consider them of sufficient importance or did not care as much about publishing them as about putting them down.

An Inveterate Reader

¶ Step into the reference rooms of your city library on a summer's day and you will stand more chance of finding examples of this extreme type there than in any other spot.

You may have thought these extreme types are difficult to locate, since the average American is a combination. But it is easy to find any of them if you look in the right places.

In every case you will find them in the very places where a study of Human Analysis would tell you to look for them.

Where to Look for Pure Types

¶ When you wish to find some pure Alimentives, go to a restaurant that is famous for its rich foods. When you want to see several extreme Thoracics, drop into any vaudeville show and take your choice from the actors or from the audience. When you are looking for pure Musculars go to a boxing match or a prize fight and you will be surrounded by them. When looking for the Osseous attend a convention of expert accountants, bankers, lumbermen, hardware merchants or pioneers.

All these types appear in other places and in other vocations, but they are certain to be present in large numbers any day in any of the above-named places.

But when you are looking for this interesting little extreme thinker-type you must go to a library. We specify the reference room of the library because those who search for fiction, newspapers and magazines are not necessarily of the pure type. And we specify a day in summer rather than in winter so that you will be able to select your subjects from amongst people who are there in spite of the weather rather than because of it.

Interested in Everything

¶ "I never saw a book without wanting to read it," said a Cerebral friend to us the other day. This expresses the interest every person of this type has in the printed page. "I never see a library without wishing I had time to go there and stay till I had read everything in it."

The Book Worm

¶ So it is small wonder that such a one becomes known early in life as a "book worm." As a little child he takes readily to reading and won't take to much else. Because we all learn quickly what we like, he is soon devouring books for older heads. "Why won't he run and play like other children?" wails Mother, and "That boy ought to be made to join the ball team," scolds Father; but "that boy" continues to keep his nose in a book.

He can talk on almost any subject—when he will—and knows pretty well what is going on in the world at an age when other boys are oblivious to everything but gymnasiums and girls.

Old for His Years

¶ The "little old man" or "little old woman" of ten is always a Cerebral child. The Alimentives are the babies of the race and never entirely grow up no matter how many years they live. But the Cerebral is born old. From infancy he shows more maturity than other children.

The "Teacher's Pet"

¶ His studiousness and tractableness lead to one reward in childhood, though it often costs him dear as a man. He usually becomes the teacher's favorite and no wonder: he always has his lessons, he gives her little trouble and is about all that keeps many a teacher at her poorly paid post.

Little Sense of Time

¶ The extreme Cerebral often has a deficient sense of time. He is less conscious of the passage of the hours than any other type. The Muscular and the Osseous often have an almost uncanny time-sense, but the extreme Cerebral man often lacks it. Forgetting to wind his watch or to consult it for hours when he does, is a familiar habit of this type.

We know a bride in Detroit whose flat looked out on a bakery and a bookstore. She told us that she used to send her Cerebral hubby across the street for the loaf of bread that was found lacking just as they were ready to sit down to dinner—only to wait hours and then have him come back with a book under his arm, no bread and no realization of how long he had been gone.

Inclined to be Unorthodox

¶ Other types tend to follow various religions—according to the individual's upbringing—but the Cerebral composes a large percentage of the unorthodox.

The Political Reformer

¶ Because all forms of personal combat are distasteful to him the pure Cerebral does not go out and fight for reform as often as the Muscular nor die for causes as often as the Osseous types.

But almost every Cerebral believes in extreme reforms of one kind or another. He is a comparatively silent but faithful member of clubs, leagues and other kinds of reform organizations. He may never star in them. He seldom cares to. But his mite is always ready when subscriptions are taken, even if he has to go without breakfast for a week to make up for it.

This type is usually sufficiently intelligent to know the world needs reforming and sufficiently conscientious to want to help to do it. He is not bound by traditions or customs as much as other types but does more of his own thinking. Without the foresight and faithfulness of the Cerebrals very few reforms could have started or have lived to finish.

The Social Nonconformist

¶ Ask any small-bodied, large-headed man if he believes in the double standard of morals, anti-suffrage, eternal punishment, saloons, or the "four hundred!" This little man with the big head may not openly challenge you or argue with you when you stand up for "things as they are," for he is a peaceable chap—but he inwardly smiles or sneers at what he considers your troglodyte ideas. He sees a day coming when babies will be named for their fathers whether the minister officiated or not; when the man who now talks about the "good old days of a wide open saloon on every corner" will himself be a hazy myth; and when society idlers will not be considered better than people who earn their livings.

The World's Pathfinder

¶ The Cerebral therefore leads the world in ideas. The world is managed by fat men, entertained by florid men, built by muscular men, opposed by bony men, but is improved in the final analysis by its thinking men.

These thinkers have a difficult time of it. They preach to deaf ears. And often they die in poverty. But at last posterity comes around to their way of thinking, abandons the old ruts and follows the trails they have blazed. Therefore many great thinkers who were unknown while alive became famous after death. More often than not, "Fame is the food of the tomb."

Indifference to Surroundings

¶ A wise man it was who said, "Let me see a man's surroundings and I will tell you what he is." The Cerebral does not really live in his house but in his head, and for that reason does not feel as great an urge to decorate, amplify or even furnish the place in which he dwells.

Step into the room of any little-bodied large-headed man and you will be struck by two facts—that he has fewer jimcracks and more journals lying around than the rest of your friends.

In the room of the Alimentive you will find cushions, sofas and "eats;" in that of the Thoracic you will find colorful, unusual things; the Muscular will have durable, solid, plain things; the Osseous will have fewer of everything but what he does have will be in order.

But the pure Cerebral's furnishings—if he is responsible for them—will be an indifferent array, with no two pieces matching. Furthermore, everything will be piled with newspapers, magazines, books and clippings.

Often Die Young

¶ "The good die young" is an old saying which may or may not be true. But there is no doubt that the extreme Cerebral type of individual often dies at an early age.

The reason is clear. An efficient but *controlled* assimilative system is the first requisite for long life, and the pure Cerebral does not have an efficient one. Moreover, he is prone to neglect what nutritive mechanism he does have, by irregular eating, by being too poor to afford wholesome foods, and by forgetting to eat at all.

Physical Assets

¶ By reason of his deficient physicality the Cerebral can not be said to possess any decided physical assets. But two tendencies which help decidedly to prolong life are under-eating and his refusal to dissipate.

It has been said many times by the best known experts that "more deaths are caused annually in America by over-eating than by any other two causes." Under-eating is a very necessary precaution but the Cerebral carries it too far.

The Cerebral, lacking a large alimentary system, is not tempted to overload his stomach or overtax his vital organs. And because he is a highly evolved type, possessing little of the instincts which are at the bottom of most dissipation, he is not addicted to late hours, wine, women or excitement.

Diseases He is Most Susceptible To

¶ Nervous diseases of all kinds most frequently afflict this type. His nervous system is supersensitive. It breaks down more easily and more completely than that of the more elemental types, just as a high-powered car is more easily wrecked than a truck.

Music He Likes

¶ "Highbrow" music is kept alive mostly by highbrows. While the other types cultivate a taste for grand opera or simulate it because it is supposedly proper, the Cerebral really enjoys it. In the top gallery at any good concert you will find many Cerebrals.

Entertainment He Prefers

¶ The serious drama and educational lectures are other favorite entertainments of the Cerebral. He cares little for vaudeville, girl-shows, or clap-trap farces.

The kind of program that keeps the fat man's smile spread from ear to ear takes the Cerebral to the box office for his money.

A Steady Patron at the Movies

¶ The Cerebral goes to the movies more than any other type save the fat man, but not for the same reasons. The large-brained, small-bodied man cares nothing for most of the recreations with which the other types amuse themselves, so the theater is almost his only diversion. It is oftentimes the only kind of entertainment within the reach of his purse; and it deals with many different subjects, in almost all of which the pure Cerebral has some interest.

Don't Laugh at Same Things

¶ But if you will notice next time you go to a movie it will be clear to you that the fat people and the large-headed people do not laugh at the same things. The pie-throwing and Cutey Coquette that convulse the two-hundred-pounder fail to so much as turn up the corners of the other man's mouth.

And the subtle things that amuse the Cerebral go over the heads of the pure Alimentives.

Cares for No Sports

¶ But the fat man and the large-brained man have one trait in common. Neither of them cares for strenuous sports. The fat man dislikes them because he is too "heavy on his feet." The Cerebral dislikes them because he is too heavy at the opposite extremity. He expends what little energy he has in mental activities so has none left for violent physical exertion.

Likes Mental Games

¶ This type enjoys quiet games requiring thought. Chess and checkers are favorites with them.

The Impersonal

¶ The Cerebral is the most impersonal of all types. While the Alimentive tends to measure everything from the standpoint of what it can do for him personally, the Cerebral tends to think more impersonally and to be interested in many things outside of his own affairs.

Lacks Pugnacity

¶ Primitive things of every kind are distasteful to the Cerebral. The instincts of digestion, sex, hunting and pugnacity are but little developed in him. He is therefore a man who likes harmony, avoids coming to blows, and goes out of his way to keep the peace. Such a man does not go hunting and seldom owns a gun. He dislikes to kill or harm any creature.

The Cleverest Crook

¶ The Cerebral is usually a naturally moral person. But when lacking in conscience, either through bad training or other causes, he occasionally turns to crime for his income. This is because his physical frailty makes it difficult for him to do heavy work, while his mentality enables him to think out ways and means of getting a living without it.

Though the clumsy criminal may belong to any type, the cleverest crooks—those who defy detection for years—always have a large element of the Cerebral in their makeup.

Big Brains in Little Jobs

¶ There are two kinds of work in the world—head work and hand work; mental and manual. If you can star in either, life guarantees you a good living. But if you are good at neither you are doomed to dependence. The Cerebral's physical frailty unfits him for the manual and unless he is school-or self-educated he becomes the sorriest of all human misfits. He falls between the two and leads a precarious existence working in the lighter indoor positions requiring the least mentality. If you will keep your eyes open you will many times note that the little waiter in the high class restaurant or hotel has a head very large for his body. Such men are much better read, have a far greater appreciation of art and literature and more natural refinement than the porky patrons they serve.

Social Assets

¶ A fine sense of the rights of others and natural modesty and refinement are the chief social assets of this type.

Social Liabilities

¶ Lack of self-expression, too great reserve and too much abstractness in conversation are the things that handicap the Cerebral. His small stature and timid air also add to his appearance of insignificance and cause him to be overlooked at social affairs.

Emotional Assets

¶ Sympathy, gentleness and self-sacrifice are other assets of this type.

Emotional Liabilities

¶ A tendency to nervous excitement and to a lack of balance are the chief emotional handicaps of this type.

Business Assets

¶ This type has no traits which can properly be called business assets. He dislikes business, is repelled by its standards and has no place in any of its purely commercial branches.

Business Liabilities

¶ His inability to "keep his feet on the ground," and his tendency to "live in the clouds" and to be generally impractical unfit this type for business life.

Domestic Strength

¶ Tenderness, consideration and idealism are the chief domestic assets of the Cerebral type.

Domestic Weakness

¶ Inability to provide for his family, incapacity for making the money necessary to meet their needs, and his tendency to spend the little he does have on impossible schemes, are what wreck the domestic life of many splendid Cerebral men. Her inability to make one dollar do the work of two is a serious handicap to the Cerebral wife or mother.

Should Aim At

¶ This man should aim at building up his body and practicalizing his mental processes.

Should Avoid

¶ The Cerebral should avoid shallow, ignorant people, speculation and those situations that carry him farther away from the real world.

His Strong Points

¶ His thinking capacity, progressiveness, unselfishness, and highly civilized instincts are the strongest points of this type.

His Weakest Points

¶ Impracticality, dreaminess, physical frailty and his tendency to plan without doing, are the traits which stand in the way of his success.

How to Deal with this Type Socially

¶ Don't expect him to be a social lion. Don't expect him to mingle with many. Invite him when there are to be a few congenial souls, and if he wanders into the library leave him alone.

How to Deal with this Type in Business

¶ Don't employ this man for heavy manual labor or where there is more arm work than head work. Give him mental positions or none.

If you are dealing with him as a tradesman, resist the temptation to take advantage of his impracticality and don't treat him as if you thought money was everything.

Remember, the chief distinguishing marks of the Cerebral, in the order of their importance, are the HIGH FOREHEAD and a PROPORTION ATELY LARGE HEAD FOR THE BODY. Any person who has these is largely of the Cerebral type no matter what other types may be included in his makeup.

To Understand Combinations

 etermine which type PREDOMINATES in a subject.

If there is any doubt in your mind about this do these four things:

1st. Note the body build—which one of the five body types (as shown in Charts 1, 3, 5, 7, 9) does he most resemble? (In doing this it will aid you if you will note whether fat, bone or muscle predominates in his bodily structure.)

2nd. Decide which of the five typical faces his face most resembles.

3rd. Decide which of the five typical hands his hands most resemble.

4th. If still undecided, note his voice, gestures and movements and they will leave no doubt in your mind as to which of these types comes first and which second.

Having decided which type predominates and which is second in him, the significance of this combination is made clear to you by the following law:

Law of Combination

¶ The type PREDOMINATING in a person determines WHAT he does throughout his life—the NATURE of his main activities.

The type which comes second in development will determine the WAY he does things—the METHODS he will follow in doing what his predominant type signifies.

The third element, if noticeable, merely "flavors" his personality.

Thus, a Cerebral-Muscular-Alimentive does MENTAL things predominantly throughout his life, but in a more MUSCULAR way than if he were an extreme Cerebral. The Alimentive element, being third down the list, will tend to make him eat and assimilate more food than he otherwise would.

CHAPTER VI

Types That Should
and Should Not Marry
Each Other

am so sorry to hear the Browns are being divorced. I have known George and Mary for years and they are as fine a man and woman as I ever saw. But they just don't seem able to get along together."

How many times you have heard something like this. And the speaker got nearer the truth than he knew. For the Georges and Marys everywhere are, on the whole, fine men and women.

Married to the Wrong One

¶ Each one is all right in himself, but merely married to the wrong person—a fact we have recognized when both George and Mary made successes of their second ventures and lived happily ever after.

Human happiness, as we have noted in the introduction to this volume, is attained only through *doing what the organism was built to do, in an environment that is favorable*. Marriage is only the attempt of two people to attain these two ends individually, mutually and simultaneously.

Difficulties of Double Harness

¶ Now, since it is almost impossible for one to achieve happiness when untrammeled and free, is it to be wondered at that so few achieve it in double harness? For the difficulties to be surmounted are doubled and the helps are halved by the presence of a running mate.

Mere Marriedness is not Mating

¶ That "two can live on less than one" is not true—but it is nearer the truth than that two can find ultimate happiness together easier than either can find an approximation of happiness alone.

This is not saying that any one who is unmated can have happiness as complete as that which comes to the rightly mated—for nothing else in life can compare with that—but they must be RIGHTLY MATED, not merely *married*.

No one who has observed or thought on this subject will deny that it is a thousand times better not to be married at all than to be married to the wrong person.

Secrets Told by Statistics

¶ Surveys of the causes for divorce during the past ten years in the United States have revealed some startling facts—facts which only prove again that Human Analysis shows us the truth about ourselves as no science has ever shown it to us before.

One of the most illuminating facts these surveys have revealed is that *only those men and women can be happy together whose natures automatically encourage each other in the doing of the things each likes to do, in the way each likes to do them.*

Inborn inclination determines the things every human being prefers to do, concerning all the fundamental activities of his life, and also the manner in which he prefers to do them. These inborn inclinations, as we have previously pointed out, are written all over us in the unmistakable language of type.

When we know a man's type we know what things he prefers to *do* in life's main experiences and *how* he prefers to do them. And we know that unless he is permitted to do approximately what he *wants* to do in approximately the *way* he prefers, he becomes unhappy and unsuccessful.

Infatuation No Guide

¶ These biological bents are so deeply embedded in every individual that no amount of affection, admiration, or respect, or passion for any other individual suffices to enable any one to go through long years doing what he dislikes and still be happy. Only in the first flush of infatuation can he sacrifice his own preferences for those of another.

After a while passion and infatuation ooze away. Nature sees to that, just as she sees to their coming in the first place. Then there return the old leanings, preferences, tendencies and cravings inherent in the type of each.

The Real "Reversion to Type"

¶ Under this urge of his type each reverts gradually but irresistibly to his old habits, doing largely what he prefers to do in the ways that are to his liking. When that day comes the real test of their marriage begins. If the distance between them is too great they can not cross that chasm, and thereafter each lives a life inwardly removed from the other.

They make attempts to cross the barrier and some of these are successful for a short while. They talk to and fro across the void sometimes; but their communings become less frequent, their voices less distinct, until at last each withdraws into himself. There he lives, in the world of his own nature—as completely separated from his mate as though they dwelt on different planets.

We Can Know

¶ "But how is one to know the right person?" you ask. By recognizing science's recent discovery to the effect that certain types can travel helpfully, happily and harmoniously together and that certain others never can.

What Every Individual Owes to Himself

¶ Every individual owes it to himself to find the right work and the right mate, because these are fundamental needs of every human being.

Lacking them, life is a failure; possessing but one of them, life is half a failure.

To obtain and apply the very fullest knowledge toward the attainment of these two great requisites should be the aim of every person.

Neglected Subjects

¶ Despite the fact that these are the most vital problems pertaining to human happiness and that every individual's life depends for its glory or defeat, joy or sorrow upon the right settlement of them—they are two of the most neglected.

Divorce Courts

¶ Our divorce courts are full of splendid men and women who are there not because they are weak or wrong, but because they stepped into nature's age-old Instinct trap without realizing where it would lead them.

These men and women who pay so heavy a price for their ignorance and blindness are *not* to blame. Most of them have been taught that to be legally bound together was sufficient guarantee of marital bliss.

But experience has shown us that there are certain kinds of people each individual can associate with in harmony and that there are those with whom he could never be happy though a hundred ministers pronounced them mated for life.

Times Will Change

¶ But the time is coming when we will select our mates scientifically, not merely sentimentally. It is also coming when we will know what every child is fitted to do by looking at him, just as we know better today than to set a shepherd dog on the trail of criminals or a bloodhound to herd sheep.

The Great Quest

¶ Instead of beclouding the significance and the sanity of life's great quest; instead of encouraging every manner of mismating as we do today, we will some day arm our children with knowledge enabling them to wisely choose their life work and their life mate.

Dolly's Dimple

¶ The fact that Dolly has a dimple may make your senses whirl but it is not sufficient basis for marriage. There are things of vastly greater importance, though of course this does not seem possible to you at the time.

Sammy's Smile

¶ And though Sammy sports a smile the gods might envy, he may not be the right man for Dolly. Even a smile that never comes off, great lubricator that it undeniably is, is not sufficient foundation for a "till-death-do-us-part" contract.

Little Things vs. Big Things

¶ When we hear of a divorce we assume that it was caused by the inability of those two people to agree upon fundamentals. We suppose that they found within themselves wide divergences of opinion, feeling or attitude regarding really worth while questions—social, religious, political or economic. We are inclined to imagine that "the little things" should take care of themselves and that only the "big things" such as these should be allowed to separate two lives, once they have been joined together.

What the Records Show

¶ Yet the exact opposite is what happens, according to the divorce records of the United States.

These records show that divorces do not arise out of differences in what we have always called the big things of life, but out of those things which we have always called the little ones.

Why He Can't Change

¶ We do not expect a husband or wife to change his religion and take on his partner's faith. We imagine this is an inherent thing more or less deeply imbedded in him and not to be altered, while we consider it only fair and right for John to give up his favorite sport, his hobby and some of his habits for Mary's sake.

At the risk of shocking the supersensitive, it must be admitted that most individuals get their religious leanings from external sources—parents, teachers, ministers, friends and especially by the accident of being born in a certain country, among a certain sect or within a certain community.

On the other hand, one's preferences in the matter of diversions are born in him, part and parcel of his very being and remain so to the end of his life. Accordingly, just as it is easier to change the frosting on a cake than to change the inside, it is easier to change a man's religion than to change his activities.

Diversion and Divorce

¶ Most of the divorces granted in America during the past ten years have been demanded, not on grounds dealing with the so-called fundamentals, but for differences regarding so-called unimportant things. And more than seventy out of every hundred divorces every year in this country are asked for on grounds pertaining to *diversion*.

In other words, more than seventy per cent of American divorces are granted because husbands and wives can not adapt themselves to each other in the matter of how they shall spend their LEISURE hours.

"People who can not play together will not work together long," said Elbert Hubbard. Human Analysis, which shows that each type tends automatically to the doing of certain things in certain ways whenever free to act, proves that this is just as literal as it sounds.

The only time we are free to act is during our leisure hours. All other hours are mortgaged to earning a living—in the accomplishment of which we often have very little outlet for natural trends. So it is only "after hours" and "over Sundays" that the masses of mankind have an opportunity to express their real natures.

Uncongenial Work Affects Marriage

¶ The less one's work permits him to do the things he enjoys the more surely will he turn to them in the hours when this restraint is removed. If such a one has a husband or wife who encourages him in the following of his natural bents during leisure hours, that marriage stands a big chance of being happy.

These two people may differ widely in their respective religious ideas—one may be a Catholic, the other a Protestant, or one a Shaker and the other a Christian Scientist—but they can build lasting happiness together.

On the other hand, two people who agree perfectly as to religious, social and political views but who can not agree as to the disposition of their leisure hours are bound for the rocks.

As the honeymoon fades, each reverts to the kind of recreation congenial to his type. If his mate is averse to his diversions each goes his own way.

The Eternal Triangle

¶ The tragedy of "the other man" and "the other woman" is not a mystery to him who understands Human Analysis. It is always the result of finding some one of kindred standards and tastes—that is, some one whose type is congenial. The Eternal Triangle arises again and again in human lives, not accidentally, but as the inevitable result of violating inexorable laws.

Law of Marital Happiness

¶ MARRIAGE SHOULD TAKE PLACE ONLY BETWEEN THOSE WHOSE FIRST TYPE-ELEMENTS ARE SUFFICIENTLY SIMILAR FOR THEM TO ENJOY THE SAME GENERAL DIVERSIONS, YET WHOSE SECOND TYPE-ELEMENTS ARE SUFFICIENTLY DISSIMILAR TO MAKE EACH STRONG WHERE THE OTHER IS WEAK.

¶ The application of the law to each of the five types will be explained in the following sections of this chapter.

Part One

THE ALIMENTIVE IN LOVE

¶ Just as each type reacts differently to all the other situations in life, each reacts differently to love.

The Alimentive, as we have pointed out, is less mature than the other types, with the Thoracic next, and so on down to the Cerebral which is the most mature of all. Because the Alimentive has rightly been called "the baby of the race;" because no extremely fat person ever really grows up, this type prefers those love-expressions natural to the immature.

The Most Affectionate Type

¶ Caressing, petting, fondling and cuddling—those demonstrations not of wild passion but of affection such as children enjoy—are most often used by Alimentive men and women when in love.

¶ Because they are inclined to bestow little attentions more or less promiscuously, they often get the reputation of being flirtatious when they are not. Such actions also are often taken by the one to whom they are directed as indicating more than the giver means.

So beware of taking the little pats of fat people too seriously. They mean well, but have the baby's habit of bestowing innocent smiles and caresses everywhere.

Why They are Loved

¶ Each type has traits peculiar to itself which tend to make others fall in love with it. In the Alimentive the outstanding trait which wins love is his sweet disposition.

The human ego is so constituted that we tend to like all interesting people who do not offer us opposition. The Alimentive is amenable, affable, agreeable. His ready smile, his tendency to promote harmony and his general geniality bring him love and keep it for him while more clever types lose it.

Millionaires Marry Them

¶ "Why does a brilliant business man marry that little fat woman who is not his equal mentally?" the world has asked many a time. Human Analysis answers it, as it answers so many of the other age-long queries about human eccentricities.

¶ The little fat woman has a sweet disposition—one of the most soothing of human attributes. The business man has enough of "brilliant" people all day. When he gets home he is rather inclined to be merely the "tired business man," and in that state nothing is more agreeable than a wife with a smile.

¶ As for fat husbands, many a wife supports them in preference to being supported by another and less agreeable man.

The Prettiest Type

¶ When a woman becomes engaged her friends all inquire, "What does he do?" but when a man's engagement is announced every one asks, "What does she look like?" So it is small wonder that men have placed prettiness near the top of the list, and the Alimentive woman is the prettiest of all types. This little fact must not be overlooked when searching for the causes which have prompted so many of the world's wealthiest men to marry them. Other men may have to content themselves with plain wives, but the man of means can pick and choose—and every man prefers a pretty wife to a plain one.

Feminine prettiness (not beauty) consists of the rose-bud mouth, the baby eyes, the cute little nose, the round cheeks, the dimpled chin, etc.—all more or less monopolized by the Alimentive type.

The "Womanly" Type

¶ The fat woman's refusal to worry keeps the wrinkles away and as long as she does not become obese she remains attractive. Her "clinging-vine" ways make men call her the most "womanly" type, and even when she tips the scales at two hundred and fifty they are still for her. Then they say "she looks so motherly."

So the fat woman goes through life more loved by men than any other type, and in old age she presents a picture of calmness and domestic serenity that is appealing to everybody.

Marry Earliest and Oftenest

¶ Being in demand, the Alimentive woman marries earlier than any other type. As a widow the same demand takes her off the marriage market while younger and brainier women pine their lives away in spinsterhood.

Look back and you will recall that it was the pretty, plump girls who had beaux earliest, married earliest, and who, even when left with several children, did not remain widows long.

Desirable Traits of Alimentive Wives

¶ Next to her sweet disposition, the traits which make the Alimentive wife most pleasant to get along with are serenity, optimism and good cooking.

Her Weaknesses

¶ Many an Alimentive wife loses her husband's love because of her too easy-going habits. Unless controlled, these lead to slovenliness in personal appearance and housekeeping.

The Alimentive Wife and Money

¶ The Alimentive wife usually has her share of the family income because she has the endearing ways that wring it out of hubby.

Sales people everywhere say, "We like to see a fat woman coming, for she usually has money, spends it freely and is easy to please."

In Disagreements

¶ What they do with their quarrels after they are through with them determines to a great extent the ultimate success of any pair's marriage. Alimentive husbands and wives bury the hatchet sooner than other types and they avoid altercations.

Lives Anywhere

¶ The Alimentive wife offers less resistance to her husband's plans than any other. So when he announces they are moving to some other neighborhood, city or state she acquiesces with better grace than other types.

Family Friends

¶ The responsibility of adding new friends to the family rests equally upon each partner in marriage. The average husband, by reason of mingling more with the world, has the greater opportunity, but every wife can and should consider that she owes it to herself, her husband and her children to contribute her quota.

Alimentive husbands and wives add their share of new acquaintances to any marriage in which they are partners. The Alimentive wife always enjoys having people in to dinner and the Alimentive husband enjoys bringing them. The warmth of hospitality in Alimentive homes brings them more friendships than come to other types.

Fat Man Also Marries Young

¶ The fat man marries young, but for a different reason than the fat woman. The fat man, as you will note, "gets a job" early in life. From that time on his services seldom go begging.

He makes a good salary earlier than other types and is therefore sooner in a position to marry.

The "Ladies' Man"

¶ Just as the fat woman is "a man's woman," so the fat man is almost invariably "a ladies' man." The fat man usually "knows women" better than any other type and it is certain that the fat woman "knows men." Her record proves it.

No Fat Bachelors

¶ Just as there are few fat "old maids," there are few fat bachelors. You can count on the fingers of one hand all the really overweight ones you ever knew.

The Best "Provider"

¶ Because he makes money easily through the various forms of his superior business qualifications, the average fat man has plenty of money for his family and likes to spend it upon them. He is the best provider of all the types. Fat people are the most lenient parents and usually over-indulge their children.

The husband who makes a habit for years of sending home crates of the first strawberries, melons and oranges of the season is a fat one every time.

Desirable Traits of Fat Husbands

¶ His generous provision for his family and the fact that he is essentially a "family man" are two desirable traits of the Alimentive husband. He depends more on his home than other types, he marries young to have a home and he is seldom farther away from it than he has to be.

It is unfortunate that the one type which makes the best "travelling man" is more inconvenienced by the absence from home than any other type would be. But he has not submitted silently. All the world knows what a "hard life" the traveling salesman leads and how he misses "the wife, the kids and the good home cooking."

Weaknesses of Alimentive Husbands

¶ The Alimentive husband has but one weakness that materially endangers his marital happiness. He is inclined to be too easy and extravagant, and not to save money.

Mates for Alimentives

¶ Because of his amenability the Alimentive can marry almost any type and be happy. But for fullest happiness, those who are predominantly Alimentive— that is, those in whom the Alimentive type comes first—should marry, as a first choice, those who are predominantly Muscular. The Muscular shares the Alimentive's ambition to "get on in the world" and at the same time adds to the union the practicality which offsets the too easy-going, lackadaisical tendencies of the Alimentive.

The second choice for the predominantly Alimentive should be the one who is predominantly Thoracic. These two types have much in common. The brilliance and speed of the Thoracic keeps the Alimentive "looking to his laurels," and thus tends to prevent the carelessness which is so great a handicap to the predominantly Alimentive.

The third choice of the predominantly Alimentive may be one who is also predominantly Alimentive, but in that case it should be an Alimentive-Muscular or an Alimentive-Cerebral.

The last type the pure Alimentive should ever marry is the pure Cerebral.

Part Two

LOVE AND THE THORACIC

¶ The Thoracic in love exhibits the same general traits which characterize him in all his other relationships.

The Most Beautiful Woman

¶ The Thoracic woman is the most beautiful type of all. She is not "pretty" like the Alimentive, but her refined features and beautiful coloring give her a distinctive appearance.

The Handsomest Man

¶ The Thoracic is also the handsomest man of all. He is tall, high-chested, wide-shouldered and has the masculine face resulting from his high-bridged, prominent nose and high cheek bones.

The Thoracic Charmer

¶ The Thoracic has more of that quality we call "charm" than any other type. Charm is largely self-expression by tactful methods. Since this type is the most self-expressive and the most tactful it possesses naturally this invaluable trait.

Both men and women of this type have an elusive, attractive something in their personalities that others do not have—a very personal appeal that makes an immediate impression. It pierces farther beneath the surface of strangers than other types do on much longer acquaintance. The Thoracic does not seem a stranger at all. His own confidences, given to you almost immediately upon meeting you, remove the barriers.

The Lure of the Thoracic

¶ There is about the Thoracic person a lure that others seldom have. You do not attempt to describe it. You say "he is just different," and he is. No other type has his spontaneity and instantaneous responsiveness.

So while the Alimentive is always liked, it is in a more mild, easy, comfortable way. The Alimentive does not stir the blood but has a strong, tender, even hold on people. The Thoracic, on the other hand, intrigues your attention, impales it, and holds it.

Love at First Sight

¶ The Thoracics fall in love at first sight much more often than other types. They also cause others to fall in love with them without preliminaries, for they pursue the object of their affections with a fire and fury that is almost irresistible.

¶ Hundreds of persons marry each year who have known each other but a few days or weeks. In every instance you will find that one of them is a Thoracic—and usually both. No other type can become so hopelessly in love on such short notice.

The Most Flirtatious

¶ The Thoracic is a born philanderer.

He does not mean to mislead or injure, but flirtation is second nature to him. This comes from the fact that flirtation, more than any other human experience, contains that adventurous, thrilling element he desires.

Overheard in Transit

¶ We overheard the following conversation in the street car the other day between two young women who occupied the seat in front of us: "I was sorry to hurt him," explained the Thoracic. "I did love him last week and I told him so, but I don't love him any more and I do love somebody else now." She really loved him—last week!

Thoracics can have a severe case of love, and get just as completely over it in a week as the rest of us get over the measles.

The Joy of Life

¶ A joy in living expresses itself in almost everything the Thoracic does, especially when he is young. Such people appear almost electrical. These are traits of great fascination and the Thoracic uses them freely upon others throughout his life.

Always Blushing

¶ His over-developed circulatory system causes the Thoracic to blush easily and often. This tendency has long been capitalized by women but is not so much enjoyed by men.

Most Easily Hurt

¶ Because of his supersensitiveness the Thoracic's feelings are more easily hurt than those of other types, as every one who has ever had a florid friend or sweetheart will remember.

They forgive quickly and completely, but every little thing said, looked, or acted by the loved one is translated in terms of the personal. Bony people especially find it difficult to understand or be tolerant of this trait in the Thoracic, because it is the exact opposite of themselves. They call the Thoracic "thin-skinned," and the Thoracic replies that the bony man has "a skin like a walrus." And each is right from his own viewpoint.

The Chivalrous Thoracic Man

¶ With his keen intuitions, his sense of the fitness of things and his trigger-like adeptness, the Thoracic man easily becomes an attentive and chivalrous companion.

Where the bony man is often oblivious to the fine points of courtesy, the Thoracic anticipates his friend's every wish and movement, picks up her handkerchief almost before she has dropped it, opens doors instantaneously and specializes in those graces dear to the heart of woman.

He is likely to do as much for the very next lady he meets just as soon as he meets her. These ready courtesies cost the Thoracic husband as many explanations as the caressing habit costs the Alimentive.

Breaches of Promise

¶ More bona fide breach of promise suits are brought against the Thoracic man than any other. He thinks rapidly, speaks almost as quickly as he thinks and about what he thinks.

Consequently many an honorable man has awakened some morning to find he has to "pay the piper" for an impulsive proposal made to a girl he would not walk across the street now to see.

Many a girl, too, when she is "in love with love" promises to marry, and the next day wonders what made her do it.

This is the type of chameleon-like girl whose vagaries and "sweet uncertainties" form the theme of many short stories, in most of which she is pictured as "the eternal feminine."

She Gets Much Attention

¶ Nevertheless, many a man prefers this creature of "a million moods" to the staid and sedate girl of other types. So the Thoracic girl seldom lacks for attention. She does not have as many intimate friends as the fat girl, for she is less comforting, and comfort is one of the first requisites of friendship. But she has a longer line of beaux dancing attendance upon her, sending her flowers, candy and messages.

The Stunning Girl

¶ Another reason why the Thoracic girl has more attention from men is that she is the most smartly-gowned of all the types. The new, the extreme, the "very latest" in women's clothes are first seen on the Thoracic girl. She is the type men call "stunning."

Men prefer companions who appear well—whom other men admire. The Thoracic woman demands the same of the men she goes about with, and for these two reasons many Thoracics marry those in whom their own type predominates.

The "Merry Widows"

¶ Make a note of the "dashing widows," you have known—those who were called "the merry widows"—and you will recall a large Thoracic element in each.

For this type of woman, unlike the home-keeping Alimentive, enjoys being a widow and remains one. She usually has many chances to remarry but her changeable, gaiety-loving nature revels in the freedom, sophistication and distinction of widowhood.

The appearance of endless youth given by her alive, responsive personality deceives the most discerning as to her age. The woman of fifty who enthralls the youths of twenty-five is usually of the Thoracic type.

Refuses to Grow Old

¶ This woman refuses to grow old, just as the Alimentive refuses to grow up. She clings to her beauty as does no other type. She it is who self-sacrificingly starves herself to retain her slenderness, who massages and exercises and "cold-creams" herself hours a day before the shrine of Eternal Youth. Her high color, "all her own," is a decided asset in this direction.

This woman devotes as much attention to her grooming at sixty as the Alimentive does at twenty. For this reason you may any day see two women of forty together, one an Alimentive and the other a Thoracic—and take the plump one to be several or many years older than the florid one.

Love the "Bright Lights"

¶ Thoracic men and women care more about "the bright lights" than other types. The Alimentive likes what he calls "a good time"—with fun and plenty of "refreshments"—but the Thoracic's idea of a good time usually includes a touch of "high life."

This all comes from his love of thrill and novelty and is innocent enough. But it leads to misunderstandings and broken homes unless the Thoracic marries the right type of person.

¶ The Osseous, for instance, has nothing in his consciousness by which to understand the desire for excitement which is so strong in the Thoracic. We have all known good wives and loving mothers whose marital happiness was destroyed because they could not compel themselves to lead the drab existence laid out for them by their bony, stony husbands. In many cases the wife, who only wanted a little innocent fun, was less to blame than her unbending spouse.

Why She Went Insane

¶ One day several years ago we drove up to a lonely farmhouse in Montana just as a tragedy was enacted. The mother was being taken to the state asylum for the insane. The seven little children watched the strange performance, unable to understand what had happened. The father, a tall, raw-boned, angular man was almost as mystified as the children.

"Crazy?" he said, "I don't believe it. Say, what did she have to go crazy about? She hasn't seen anything to excite her. Why, she's not been off this farm for twenty years!"

The "Gay Devil" Husband

¶ The same thing happens every day between severe, bony wives and their florid, frolicking husbands. "She is a perfect housekeeper and a good wife" exclaim her friends—"why should her husband spend his evenings away from home?" These questions will continue to be asked until we realize that being "a good housekeeper and a good wife" does not fill the bill with a Thoracic man. A wife who will leave the dinner dishes in the kitchen sink occasionally and run away with him for a "lark" on a moment's notice is the kind that retains the love of her florid husband. A husband who is willing to leave his favorite magazine, pipe, and slippers to take her out in the evening is the kind a Thoracic woman likes. She even prefers a "gay devil" to a "stick"—as she calls the slow ones.

Makes Him Jealous

¶ The Thoracic man wants his wife to look well and be pleasing but no husband wants his wife to be irresistibly attractive to other men. So it often happens that the Thoracic woman causes her husband much jealousy.

Her youthful actions and distinctive dressing make her a magnet for all eyes. If he happens to be too different in type to understand her naturalness and pure-mindedness in this he often suffers keenly. Sometimes he causes *her* to suffer for it when they get home.

Human Analysis makes us all more tolerant of each other. It enables us to know why people act as they do, and, best of all, that they mean well and not ill most of the time.

Dislikes the Monotonous

¶ The Thoracic, you will remember, dislikes monotony. Everything savoring of routine, sameness—the dead level—wears on him.

Three meals a day three hundred and sixty-five days in a year, with the same person, in the same room, at the same table, is unspeakably irksome to him. He may love that other person with completeness and constancy, but he occasionally demands what Bernard Shaw calls "domestic change of air."

"My Wife's Gone to the Country," was the biggest song hit of its year because there were so many florid men who understood just how that man felt!

¶ The florid wife is as loving as any other but she heaves a sigh of relief and invites her women friends in for a party when John goes away on business.

Not Easy to Live With

¶ Thoracic husbands or wives are not as easy to live with as the Alimentive. They are too affectable, too susceptible to sudden changes of mood. They live alternately on the crest of the wave and in the depths, and rob the home of that serenity which is essential to harmony.

Impulsive tendencies which made the sweetheart adorable are less attractive in the wife. And hubby's hair-trigger temperament she now calls just plain temper.

Desirable Traits of Thoracics

¶ That they are the most charming in manner, the most tasteful in dress and the most entertaining of any type constitute the traits which make the Thoracic husband or wife desirable and attractive.

Live Beyond Means

¶ Husbands and wives of this type present this marital problem however: they tend to live beyond their means. The husband in such a case seldom confides the true state of his financial affairs to his wife while the Thoracic wife, bent on making the best possible appearance, finds it almost impossible to trim down expenditures to fit the family purse.

The habit of entertaining extravagantly and almost constantly also costs the Thoracic household dear.

¶ The desire on the part of a Thoracic husband or wife to move frequently from that particular house, neighborhood, or city presents another difficulty.

Should Marry Own Type

¶ For the reasons stated above and throughout this work, the predominantly Thoracic person should marry his own type as first choice. No other can understand his impulsiveness.

His second choice should be a person predominantly of the Alimentive type. The Alimentive is more like the Thoracic than any other, and in the places where they differ the Alimentive gives in with better grace than other types.

The third choice may be a predominantly Muscular person. In the latter case, however, the Muscular should have either Thoracic or Alimentive tendencies combined with his muscularity.

Because they are so different as to be almost opposites, and therefore unable to understand each other, the last person the Thoracic should marry is the Osseous.

Part Three

MARRIAGE AND MUSCULARS

¶ The Muscular does not marry early like the Alimentive nor hastily like the Thoracic. His is a practical nature and his practicality is expressed here as in everything else. Back of his Marriage you will often find some of the same practical reasons that prompt his other activities.

Marries Between Twenty-five and Thirty-five

¶ Most Musculars are still unmarried at twenty-five when their Alimentive friends have families and when their Thoracic ones have had a divorce or two. But few Musculars are unmarried at thirty-five, though at that age their Osseous and Cerebral friends are often still single.

The Muscular does not marry on nothing, and as he does not star in any line of work as early in life as the Alimentive or Thoracic he does not have the means to marry as early in life as they. But he is a splendid worker, gets something to do and does it fairly well.

The Alimentive spends too much on food and other comforts and the Thoracic too much on luxuries, but the Muscular, while not mercenary, saves a larger portion of his income.

Make "Sensible" Marriages

¶ So at somewhere around thirty the Muscular is prepared to establish a home. By that time he has lived past the rash stage and selects a mate as much like himself as possible, in order not to be thwarted in his aims for "getting somewhere in the world"—aims which dominate this type all his life.

A Mate for Wearing Qualities

¶ This type selects his mate as he selects his clothes—for wearing quality. He prefers plain, simple people, for he is plain and simple himself. They are not carried off their feet by impulse as are some of the other types. They therefore choose wives and husbands whose lovable qualities show signs of durability.

The Most Positive Lover

¶ The Muscular makes love almost as strenuously as he does everything else. He does not do it especially gracefully like the Thoracic, nor caressingly like the Alimentive, but intensely and in dead earnest. He does not cut short the courtship like the Thoracic, nor extend it for years like the Osseous, but marries as soon as the practical requirements can be met.

The Alimentive is the most affectionate in love and the Thoracic the most flirtatious, but the Muscular is the most positive.

The Fatal Handicap

¶ The Muscular has more strong traits than any other type from the marital point of view, but he has one weakness of such magnitude that it often counterbalances them. His pugnacity causes him to give way frequently to violent outbursts of anger. In them he says bitter things that are almost impossible to forgive.

This type's chief handicap in all his relations is his tendency to fight too quickly, to say too much when angry, and thus to make enemies.

In marriage this is a serious handicap which loses many an otherwise ideal husband or wife the chance for happiness.

Another Muscular trait which makes life difficult for his mate is his tendency to be so generous with outsiders that his family suffers.

Also this type of husband or wife is inclined to sacrifice the social side of family life to work and thus widen the distance between husband and wife as the years go on.

Desirable Traits

¶ Working capacity, generosity and squareness are qualities making for the success of the Muscular marriage.

The Muscular wife, more often than any other, helps earn the living when things go wrong financially.

The Muscular usually dislikes flirtations and gives his mate little anxiety on this score.

Mates for Musculars

¶ The Muscular has four choices in the selection of a mate. There is but one type he should never marry and that is the Osseous. The stubborness of the Osseous, when pitted against the Muscular's pugnacity, causes constant warfare. The predominantly Muscular person should choose a mate who is also predominantly Muscular. No other type aids him in the practical affairs of the family's future. But it is well for him when this Muscular has decided Cerebral tendencies. Second choice for the Muscular is a mate predominantly Cerebral. The Muscular in this case furnishes the brawn to work out the plans made by the brain of the Cerebral, and the combination is one that stands a good chance of happiness. Third choice is the Thoracic, and fourth choice the Alimentive.

Part Four

THE OSSEOUS IN LOVE

¶ Bring to mind all the men and women you have known who waited ten, twenty or thirty years for the one they had given their hearts to. You will recall that they all had large bones or large joints for their bodies. Such people are always predominantly Osseous.

The loved one may marry but the bony man or woman remains faithful; it must be the one they want or none.

The Riddle Solved

¶ This fact accounts for some of the incongruous matches in middle or later life of old friends who seem to be unfitted to each other. Often one of them has waited many years for the other to consent, for children to grow up, or for Death to clear the way.

One Lover Through Life

¶ Osseous men and women are so constituted that it is practically impossible for them to love many times during a lifetime.

Bony people, even when young, have fewer sweethearts than other types. The large-boned boy or girl is usually ill at ease in the presence of the other sex, avoids social affairs, and does not attract love as early in life as other types do.

They suffer keenly from the near-ostracism resulting from this, but are powerless to change it.

Live Apart from Others

¶ Because they live more or less apart from their fellows, even as children, and tend to withdraw into themselves, the Osseous see little of the other sex, learn little about it and come to think of it as unapproachable.

138

As we have seen, the Alimentive feels at ease with the other sex, the Thoracic charms them, the Muscular cultivates them when he is in earnest, but the Osseous avoids them. If he does not marry he becomes more and more awkward in their presence as he grows older. Such a person will often go a block out of his way to avoid meeting a person of the opposite sex.

Marries Less Often

¶ This naturally leads to the unmated life which characterizes so many men and women of the Osseous type.

We asked you to recall the one or two Alimentive bachelors and spinsters you ever knew, the three or four Thoracics and the not more than half a dozen Musculars who didn't marry. But it will take some time to enumerate the Osseous people you know who have never married. This type constitutes a very large proportion of the unmarried.

Most Difficult to Live With

¶ When the Osseous does marry he is the most difficult of all types to live with, because he is inclined to be immovable and unbending.

To give and take has long been considered the secret of happy marriage and certainly is one of them. But this type finds it almost impossible to adapt himself to his mate. He wants everything in a certain way at a certain time and for a certain purpose. Whoever opposes him is pretty ruthlessly handled.

Another marital liability of this type is his disinclination and inability to make new friends. He contributes to the family circle only those few intimates he has had for years.

Likes to Dominate

¶ The Osseous is inclined to dominate and often to domineer over his mate and over his family in general. This is as true of the women as of the men. As we have seen, type and not sex is what causes the big distinctions between people.

The Hen-Pecked Husband

¶ Whenever you see a hen-pecked husband look at his wife. You will always find that she has either large joints, large bones or a square jaw.

Many times we have heard men declare "they would show such a wife how to act," but unless they could change her boniness they would find it difficult to "show her" much of anything.

The reason the husband of such a woman seldom resists is because he is nine times out of ten an Alimentive or a Cerebral—types that prefer to be bossed rather than to boss.

The same combination is usually present when the husband dominates the wife. He is almost invariably bony and she is either Alimentive or Cerebral. And other women say, "I'd like to show such a husband what I would do if he tried to tyrannize over ME as he does over her!" But such a woman often prefers a husband who relieves her of the responsibility of decisions, and two such people sometimes lead surprisingly happy lives together.

Mates for the Osseous

¶ Therefore the type best fitted to live in harmony with the predominantly Osseous is the predominantly Alimentive. Second choice is the predominantly Cerebral, for the reasons stated above. There is no third choice.

The pure Osseous and pure Thoracic should not marry because they are too far removed from each other in all their tendencies ever to understand each other.

The one type the pure Osseous should never mate with is his own. Nothing but trouble results when two of the extreme bony type marry, for each has definite views, desires and preferences—and neither can give in.

Part Five

LOVE AND THE CEREBRAL

¶ The Cerebral type takes most of his love out in dreaming. He is as impractical about his affections as about all else and often nothing but hopes come of it. Next to the Osseous he marries less frequently than any other type.

Head and Heart in the Clouds

¶ The Cerebral often remains single because he can not come down to earth long enough to propose, or if he does he is so gentle and timid about it the girl is afraid to trust her life to him.

Timidity His Curse

¶ Timidity costs the Cerebral man most of the good things he could otherwise get out of life. He is almost afraid to fall in love, afraid to speak after he does and afraid to face the hostile world with two lives on his hands.

Women Like Him

¶ The average woman likes the Cerebral type of man but seldom loves or adores him. His helplessness appeals to her motherly sympathy.

Can Not Buffet the World

¶ But women are afraid to marry the extreme type even when the feeling he prompts is more than mere protectiveness. They know he can not buffet the world for them and their offspring.

So, even when they love him best they usually marry the fat salesman, the Muscular worker who always has a good job, the Thoracic promoter who promises luxury, or the Osseous man who won't take "No" for an answer.

Always Leap Year for Him.

¶ When this type of man does marry it is often due as much to her proposal as his. He is especially aided in his courtship if "she" happens to be a quick-spoken Thoracic, a straight-from-the-shoulder Muscular, or one of those determined Osseous girls.

The Much-Loved Cerebral Woman

¶ The Cerebral woman is more fortunate in achieving marriage than the Cerebral man. The impracticality which so seriously handicaps him, since the husband is supposed to support the family, is not quite so much of a handicap to her.

Men who love her at all, love her for her tenderness, conscientiousness and delicacy and deem it a pleasure to work for her, and she is one type of woman who usually appreciates it.

The Cerebral's Weaknesses

¶ The tendency to dream his life away instead of doing tangible things that assist in the progress of the family is the greatest marital handicap of the Cerebral type.

Inability to make money results directly from this, and since money is so important in the rearing and educating of children, those who can not get it are bound to face hardship and disillusionment.

The Saddest Sight

¶ The most pathetic sight to be seen anywhere is that of the delicate, intellectual man who loves his family dearly, has the highest ideals and yet is unable to provide for them.

When Love Flies Out the Window

¶ "When poverty comes in the door love flies out the window" is a saying as old as it is sad.

¶ And it is as true as it is both old and sad.

Despite the philosophers—who are all Cerebrals themselves!—love should grow in sheltered soil, protected from the buffetings of wind and storm. Without means no man can provide this protection. Happy marriage, as we have seen, is based on the cultivation of the strong points and the submergence of the weak ones of each partner. Poverty does more to bring out the worst in people and conceal the best than anything else in the world. So, although this type is high-minded, more idealistic in his love than any other type and has fewer of the lower instincts, he makes less of a success of marriage than any other type.

Mates for the Cerebral

¶ Because he lives in his mind and not in his external world the predominantly Cerebral must marry one who also is predominantly Cerebral.

The reading of books, attendance at good plays, and the study of great movements constitute the chief enjoyments of this type and if he has a mate who cares nothing for these things his marriage is bound to be a failure.

The Cerebral he marries should, however, be inclined to the Muscular also.

Second choice for this type is the predominantly Muscular and third choice is the Osseous. The firmness of the latter is often a desirable element in the combination, for the Cerebral does not mind giving the reins over to his Osseous mate; he does not like driving anyhow.

The last type of all for the pure Cerebral to marry is the pure Alimentive because it is farthest removed from his own type. These two have very little in common.

Remember, in marriage, TYPE is not a substitute for LOVE. Both are essential to ideal mating. People contemplating matrimony are like two autoists planning a long journey together, each driving his own car. Whether they can make the same speed, climb the same grades "on high" and be well matched in general, depends on the TYPE of these two cars. But it takes LOVE to supply the gas, the self-starters and the spark plugs!

CHAPTER VII

Vocations For Each Type

"Fame and Failure"

The masses of mankind form a vast pyramid. At the very tip-top peak are gathered the few who are famous. In the bottom layer are the many failures. Between these extremes lie all the rest—from those who live near the ragged edge of Down-and-Out-Land to those who storm the doors of the House of Greatness.

Again, between these, and making up the large majority, are the myriads of laborers, clerks, small business men, housekeepers—that myriad-headed mass known as "the back bone of the world."

Yet the great distance from the lower layer to the tip-top peak is not insurmountable. Many have covered it almost overnight.

A Favorite Fallacy

¶ For fame is not due, as we have been led to believe, solely to years of plodding toil. A thousand years of labor could never have produced an Edison, a Marconi, a Curie, a Rockefeller, a Roosevelt, a Wilson, a Bryan, a Ford, a Babe Ruth, a Carpentier, a Mary Pickford, a Caruso, a Spencer or an Emerson.

Fame's Foundation

¶ The reserved seat in the tip-top peak of the pyramid is procured only by him who has *found his real vocation.*

To such a one *his* work is not hard. No hours are long enough to tire his body; no thought is difficult enough to weary his mind; to him there is no day and no night, no quitting time, no Saturday afternoons and no Sundays. He is at the business for which he was created—and all is play.

Edison Sleeps Four Hours

¶ Thomas A. Edison so loves his work that he sleeps an average of less than four hours of each twenty-four. When working out one of his experiments he forgets to eat, cares not whether it is day or night and keeps his mind on his invention until it is finished.

Yet he has reached the age of seventy-four with every mental and physical faculty doing one hundred per cent service—and the prize place in the tip-top peak of the Wizards of the World is his! He started at the very bottom layer, an orphan newsboy. He made the journey to the pinnacle because early in life he found his vocation.

Failures Who Became Famous

¶ Each one of the world's great successes was a failure first.

It is interesting to note the things at which some of them failed. Darwin was a failure at the ministry, for which he was educated. Herbert Spencer was a failure as an engineer, though he struggled years in that profession. Abraham Lincoln was such a failure at thirty-three as a lawyer that he refused an invitation to visit an old friend "because," he wrote, "I am such a failure I do not dare to take the time."

Babe Ruth was a failure as a tailor. Hawthorne was a failure as a Custom House clerk when he wrote the "Scarlet Letter." Theodore Roosevelt was a failure as a cowboy in North Dakota and gave up his frontiering because of it.

These men were failures because they tried to do things for which they were not intended. But each at last found his work, and when he did, it was so easy for him it made him famous.

Play, Not Work, Brings Fame

¶ Fame comes only to the man, or woman, who loves his work so well that it is not work but play. It comes only to him who does something with marvellous efficiency. Work alone can not produce that kind of efficiency.

Outdistancing Competition

¶ Fame comes from doing one thing so much better than your competitors that your results stand out above and beyond the results of all others. Any man who will do efficiently any one of the many things the world is crying for can place his own price upon his work and get it. He can get it because the world gladly pays for what it really wants, and because the efficient man has almost no competition.

Efficiency Comes from Enjoyment

¶ But here's the rub. You will never do anything with that brilliant efficiency save what you LIKE TO DO. Efficiency does not come from duty, or necessity, or goading, or lashing, or anything under heaven save ENJOYMENT OF THE THING ITSELF.

Nothing less will ever release those hidden powers, those miraculous forces which, for the lack of a better name, we call "genius."

Knowing What are *Not* Your Vocations

¶ Elimination of what are distinctly NOT your vocations will help you toward finding those that ARE. To that end here are some tests which will clear up many things for you. They will help you to know especially whether or not the vocations you have been contemplating are fitted to you.

How to Test Yourself

¶ Whenever you are considering your fitness for any vocation, ask yourself these questions:

Self-Question 1—Am I considering this vocation chiefly because I would enjoy the things it would bring—such as salary, fame, social position or change of scene?

If, in your heart, your answer is "Yes," this is not a vocation for you.

The Movie Hopeful

¶ The above test can best be illustrated by the story of a young woman who wanted to be told that she had ability to act. "I am determined to go into the movies," she told us. "Do you think I would be a success?"

"When you picture yourself in this profession what do you see yourself doing?" we asked.

"Oh, everything wonderful," she replied. "I see myself driving my own car—one of those cute little custom-made ones, you know—and wearing the most stunning clothes and meeting all those big movie stars—and living all the year round in California!"

"Is that all you ever see yourself doing?" we inquired.

"Yes—but isn't that enough?"

"All but one—the acting."

She then admitted that in the eight years she had been planning to enter the movies she had never once really visualized herself acting, or studying any part, or doing any work—nothing but rewards and emoluments.

Pleasure or Pay?

Self-Question 2—Knowing the requirements of this vocation—its tasks, drudgeries, hours of work, concentration and kind of activity—would I choose to follow them in preference to any other kind of activity even if the income were the same?

*Would I do these things for the **pleasure** of doing them and not for the **pay**?*

If, in your heart, you can answer "Yes" to these questions, your problem is settled; you will succeed in that vocation. For you will so enjoy your work that it will be play. Being play, you will do it so happily that you will get from it new strength each day.

Because you are doing what you were built to do, you will think of countless improvements, inventions, ways of marketing them. This will promote you over the others who are there only for the pay envelope; it will raise your salary; it will eventually and inevitably take you to the top.

A man we know aptly illustrates this point. He was a bookkeeper. He had held the same position for twenty-three years and was getting $125 a month. He had little leisure but used all he did have—evenings, Saturday afternoons, Sundays and his ten-day vacations—making things.

In that time he had built furniture for his six-room house—every kind of article for the kitchen, bathroom and porch. And into everything he had put little improving touches such as are not manufactured in such things.

We convinced him that his wife was not the only woman who would appreciate these step-saving, work-reducing, leisure-giving conveniences. He finally believed it enough to patent some of his inventions, and today he is a rich man.

Of "Your Own Accord"

¶ One more question will shed much light on the matter of your talents. Here it is:

*Self-Question 3—Do I tend to follow, of my own accord, for the sheer joy of it, the **kinds of activity** demanded by this vocation which I am contemplating?*

If you do not you will never succeed in this line of work.

Thought it Would Do Him Good

¶ One incident will serve to illustrate the foregoing test. A young man asked us if he could succeed as a public speaker. He had decided to become a lecturer and had spent two years studying for that work.

"Do you enjoy talking? Do you like to explain and expatiate? When out with others do you furnish your share of the conversation or a little more?" were the questions we put to him.

To all of the questions he answered "No."

"But I thought this was just the line of work I ought to go into," he explained, "I have always been diffident and I thought the training would do me good."

Life Pays the Producer

¶ Expecting the world to pay you handsomely while remaking you is short-sighted, to say the least. The public schools are free, like life's education, but you don't get a salary for attending them.

To be a success you must PRODUCE something out of the ordinary for the world. And you will produce nothing unusual save what your particular organism was built to produce. To know what this is, classify the kind of activities you "take to" naturally. You can be a star in some line that calls for those activities. You will never succeed in any calling which demands the opposite kinds of activities or reactions.

The Worst Place for Her

¶ A few years ago, in San Francisco, a young woman came to us for vocational advice. She had decided to find an opening in a silk-importing establishment, for none of whose duties she was qualified. When asked how she happened to hit upon the thing for which she unquestionably had no ability, she said:

"I thought it would give me a world outlook (which I need); compel me to learn fabrics (something I think every woman ought to know); force me to attend to details (which I have always hated but which I must learn to master); and because it would bring me into contact with people (I dislike them but think I should learn to deal with them)."

When Considering a Position

¶ When a position is being considered the questions an applicant should be asking himself are, "What must I do in this position? Am I qualified? Can I make good? Do I like the activities demanded by this position?"

But ninety-nine out of every hundred applicants for a vacancy ask no question of themselves whatever, and only one of anybody else. That question is to the employer and it is only four words: "*What does it pay?*"

He overlooks the fact that if the salary involved is large enough to be attractive he will soon be severed from it unless he makes good. He also forgets that if the salary is small he can force it to grow if he is big enough himself.

If the particular task he is considering does not warrant a large salary, his employers will find one for him that does if he shows he has ability.

Every business in the world is looking for people who can do a few things a trifle better than the mass of people are doing them today, and whenever they find them they pay them well—because it pays THEM in the long run.

The Big-Salaried Men

¶ Don't be afraid that you may develop ability and then find no market for it. The only jobs that have to go begging are the big-salaried ones, because the combination of intelligence and efficiency is not easy to find. The men who are drawing from $10,000 to $50,000 a year are not supermen. They are not very different from anybody else. But they found a line that fitted their particular talents, and they went ahead cultivating those talents without asking for everything in advance.

Looking for "Chicken Feed"

¶ While touring through the Rockies last summer we came one day to a log shack perched on the mountain-side near the road. In the back-yard was the owner, just ready to feed his chickens. As he flung out the grain they came from every direction, crowding and jostling each other and frantically pecking for the tiny morsels he threw on the ground. Several dozen flocked around him. But three or four stayed on the outer edge, ready to scamper for the big grains he threw now and then amongst the boulders up on the hillside.

"I do that just to see them use their heads," he explained. "People are just like that. They rush for the little chances where all the competition is, instead of staying out where they can see a big chance when it comes."

Life is full of opportunities for every person who will consult his own capacities and *aim for the big chance.*

Causes of Misfits

¶ Various influences are responsible for the misfit, chief amongst which are his loving parents. Many fathers and mothers, with the best intentions in the world, urge their children to enter vocations for which they have no natural fitness whatever. These same parents often discourage in their children the very talents which, if permitted to develop, would make them successful.

Such a child has small chance in the world if it happens that his parents are sufficiently well-to-do to hold the purse strings on his training. Not until he has failed at the work they choose for him will such parents desist. When they finally allow him to take to the work he prefers they are usually surprised to see how clever he is.

But if he does not succeed at it they should bear in mind that it is doubtless due to their having cheated him out of his priceless youth—the years when the mind is moldable, impressionable and full of inspiration.

Poverty's One Advantage

¶ In this situation alone does the child of poverty-ridden parents have greater opportunities than the child of the well-to-do. He at least chooses his own work, and this is one more little reason why the world's most successful men so often come from the ranks of the poor.

"Ruined by too much mothering and fathering" is a verdict we would frequently render if we knew the facts.

Richard and Dorothy

¶ One instance in which Fate took a hand was very interesting. A New York widow, whose husband had left his large fortune entirely to her, nursed definite ambitions for her son and daughter. Richard, she had decided, should become a stock-raiser and farmer on the several-thousand-acre ranch they owned in Texas. Dorothy should study art in Paris.

But it so happened that Richard and Dorothy disliked the respective vocations laid out for them, while each wanted to do the very thing the other was being driven to do. Richard was small, dark, sensitive, esthetic—and bent on being an artist. Dorothy, who was six feet in her stockings, laughed at art and wanted to be a farmer.

But mother was obdurate and mother held the family purse. So, in the spring of 1914, Dorothy was sent to Paris to study the art Richard loved, and Richard was sent to the Texas ranch that Dorothy wanted.

Then the War broke and Dorothy hurried from Paris to avoid German shells, while Richard enlisted to escape the Texas ranch. Dorothy, in her element at last, took over the ranch (of which Richard had made a failure), turned it into one vast war garden, became a farmerette and is there now—a shining success.

Richard got to Paris during the War and when it closed refused to come home. He wrote his mother that the war had taught him he could earn his own living—an accomplishment he is achieving today with his art. The mother herself is happier than she ever was before, and proud of her children's success.

Three Kinds of Parents

¶ Parents can be divided into three classes—those who over-estimate their children, those who under-estimate their children, and those who do not estimate them at all.

The great majority are in the first group. This accounts for the fact that most fathers and mothers are disillusioned, as their children, one by one, fall short of their cherished hopes.

Those who under-estimate their children are in that small group—of parents who live to be happily surprised at their achievements.

The best parents of all are those who allow their children to follow their natural talents.

Don'ts for Parents

¶ Don't push your child into any vocation he dislikes.

Don't be like the parents we dined with recently. As we sat around the table they pointed out their four children as follows: "There's Georgie—we're going to make a doctor of him. Our best friend is a doctor. We'll make a lawyer out of Johnnie. There's been a lawyer in the family for generations. Jimmie is to be a minister. We thought it was about time we had one of them in the family."

"What about Helen?" we asked.

"Oh, Helen—why, she's going to marry and have a nice home of her own."

Any student of Human Analysis would have recognized that of this quartet of children not one was being directed into the right vocation. He would have seen that the square-jawed Muscular Jimmie would make a much better lawyer than a minister; that little Johnnie should be a teacher or a lecturer; that fat Georgie was born for business instead of medicine; and that Helen had more ability than any of her brothers.

The Woman Misfit

¶ Too many parents have gone on the theory that belonging to the female sex was a sure indication of home-making, mothering, housekeeping abilities.

The commercial world is full of women who have starved, wasted and shriveled their lives away behind counters, desks and typewriters when they were meant for motherhood and wifehood.

The homes of the land are also full of women who, with the brains and effort they have given to scrubbing, washing and cooking, could have become "captains of industry."

The Sealed Parcel

¶ If you are a parent don't allow yourself to set your heart on any particular line of work for your children. Your child is a sealed parcel and only his own tendencies, as they appear during youth, can tell what that parcel really contains.

Allow these traits to unfold naturally, normally and freely. Don't complicate your own problem by trying to advise him too soon. Don't praise certain professions. Children are intensely suggestible. The knowledge that father and mother consider a certain profession especially desirable oftentimes influences a child to waste time working toward it when he has no real ability for it. Every hour of youth is precious and this wastage is unspeakably expensive.

On the other hand, do not attempt to prejudice your child *against* any profession. Don't let him think, for instance, that you consider overalls a badge of inferiority, or a white collar the mark of superiority. Many a man in blue denim today could buy and sell the collar-and-cuff friends of his earlier years. The size of a man's laundry bill is no criterion of his income.

Popular Misconceptions

¶ Other parents make the equally foolish mistake of showing their dislike of certain professions. Not long ago we heard a father say in the presence of his large family, "I don't want any of my boys to be lawyers. Lawyers are all liars. Ministers are worse; they're all a bunch of Sissies. Doctors are all fakes. Actors are all bad eggs; and business is one big game of cheat or be cheated. I'm going to see that every boy I've got becomes a farmer."

Misdirected Mothering

¶ A very unfortunate case came to our attention several years ago. In Chicago a mother brought her eighteen-year-old son to us for vocational counsel. "I am determined that James shall be a minister," she said. "My whole happiness depends upon it. I have worked, slaved and sacrificed ever since his father died that he might have the education for it. Now I want you to tell James to be a minister."

We refused to take the case, explaining that our analyses didn't come to order but had to fit the facts as we found them. She still insisted upon the analysis. It revealed the fact that James was deficient mentally, save in one thing. His capacity for observing was lightning-like in its swiftness and microscopic in its completeness. And his capacity for judging remote motives from immediate actions was uncannily accurate.

He was a human ferret, as had been proven many times during his boyhood. At one time the jewelry store in which he worked as a shipping clerk lost a valuable necklace, and after the police of Chicago had failed to find a clew, James' special ability was reported and he was given a week's vacation to work on the case. He took the last three days for a long-desired trip to Milwaukee. He had landed the thief in the first four. We told the mother that her boy's ability was about the farthest removed from the ministerial that could well be imagined, but that he would make an excellent detective.

"I shall never permit it!" she cried. "His father was a policeman. I distrust that whole class of people! I am taking James to the theological seminary tomorrow"—and away she went with him. Two months later she came to us in great distress. She had received a letter from the Dean saying James had attended but one day's classes. Then he had announced that he was going home. Instead he had cultivated a gang of underworld crooks for the purpose of investigating their methods and had gotten into serious trouble.

Nevers for All

¶ Never choose a vocation just because it looks *profitable*. It won't bring profits to you long unless you are built for it.

Never choose a vocation just because it looks *easy*. No work will be easy for you except that which Nature intended for you.

Never choose a vocation just because it permits the wearing of *good clothes*. You need more than a permit; you need ability.

Never choose a vocation just because the *hours are short*. You can't fool employers that way. They also know they are short, and pay you accordingly. The extra play these leisure hours give you will amount to nothing but loss to you ten years hence.

Never choose a vocation just because it is *popular* or *sounds interesting*.

"I am going to be a private secretary," said a young woman near us at the theater recently.

"What will you have to do?" asked her friend.

"Oh, I don't know," the girl answered, "but it sounds so fascinating, don't you think?"

Never turn your back on a profession just because it is *old-fashioned, middle class or ordinary*. If you have talents fitting you for such vocations you are lucky, for these are the ones for which there is the greatest demand. Demand is a big help. If you can add a new touch to such a one you are made.

Why She Taught German

¶ Never choose a vocation just because your *friends* are in it, nor refuse another just because your worst enemy is in it.

Two friends come to mind in this connection. One is a splendid woman we knew at college. She became a German teacher and up to the outbreak of the War had an instructorship in a western state university. The elimination of German lost her the position.

"Why did you ever choose German, anyhow, Ruth?" we asked her. "Your abilities lie in such a different direction."

"Because my favorite teacher in high school taught German," she replied.

Enemies and Engineering

¶ An opposite case is that of a friend of ours who has worked in an uncongenial profession for thirty years. "You were meant for engineering, Tom," we told him. "With all the leanings you had in that direction, how did it happen you didn't follow it?"

"Because the man who cheated my father out of all he had was an engineer!" he said.

Never choose a new vocation just because you are *restless*. You will be more so if you get into the wrong one.

The "Society" Delusion

¶ Never choose a vocation just because it promises *social standing*. The entree it gives will fail you unless you make good. And social standing isn't worth much anyhow. When you are in the work for which you were born you won't worry about social standing. It will come to you then whether you want it or not. And when it does you will care very little about it.

The Entering Wedge

¶ Never take a certain job *for life* just because people are *dependent* upon you. Save enough to live one month without a job, preparing yourself meanwhile for an entering wedge into a vocation you do like. Then take a smaller-paying place if necessary to get started. If you really like the work you will do it so well you will promote yourself. You owe it to those who are dependent upon you to do this.

Jack of All Trades

¶ Never do anything just to show you *can*. Don't let your versatility tempt you into following a number of lines of work for the purpose of demonstrating your ability. Versatility can be the greatest handicap of all; it tempts you to neglect intensive study, to flit, to become a "jack of all trades and master of none."

Only Three Kinds of Work

¶ There are but three general classes of work. They are:

> WORK WITH PEOPLE;
> WORK WITH THINGS;
> WORK WITH IDEAS.

Each individual is fitted by nature to do one of these *better* than the others and there will be one class for which he has the *least* ability. In the other one of the three he might make a mediocre success. Every individual should find a vocation furnishing that one of these three kinds of work for which he has the *greatest* ability. Then he should go into the particular *branch* of that vocation which is best adapted to his personality, training, education, environment and experience.

Part One

VOCATIONS FOR ALIMENTIVES

¶ As stated in Chapter I, Alimentives are born for business. They can sell almost anything in the line of food, clothing, or shelter because they are so interested in them themselves they can make them interesting to others. They like money for the comforts which money alone can bring and business furnishes a wider field for money-making than any other. So the Alimentive likes the commercial world for itself and for what it brings him.

Sells Things to People

¶ The Alimentive can deal with both people and things, but it should be in the capacity of selling the things to the people.

Chances for Money-Making

¶ The Alimentives have the greatest opportunities today for making fortunes and many of the multi-millionaires of America are combinations of this type with the Cerebral. This is due to the fact that the world must be fed, clothed and sheltered and the Alimentive, more than any other type, excels in the marketing, manufacturing and merchandizing of these things.

A Good Overseer

¶ The Alimentive makes an excellent overseer also. He is so genial, likable and yet so bent on saving himself work that he can get more work out of others than can any other type.

So he succeeds as a foreman, supervisor, boss, superintendent, manager and sales department head.

Capitalizes His "Comfort" Instincts

¶ The Alimentive loves comforts. He feels he must have them. Because any man's success will be found to lie in the direction which most nearly satisfies his basic instincts, the Alimentive succeeds by making "the good things of life" look so interesting to others they are willing to buy them from him at the best prices.

The Alimentively Inclined

¶ Every man who is largely Alimentive in type can sell commodities or oversee the work of others. Every woman who is largely Alimentive can also sell the same commodities, oversee the work of others in her department and become a good cook.

Things to Avoid

¶ The Alimentive should avoid vocations dealing exclusively with ideas. Books are almost the only things an Alimentive can not sell successfully. This is due to the fact that he is not as interested in ideas as in things, and the things he is interested in—food and comforts—are the farthest removed from books.

Partners to Select

¶ When he goes into partnership the Alimentive should endeavor to do so with a practical Muscular, a clever Thoracic or another Alimentive.

Partners and Employees to Avoid

¶ He should avoid as partners the pure Cerebrals and the pure Osseous. The former are too high brow and visionary for him, and the Osseous are too critical of his easy ways.

Bosses to Avoid

¶ The Alimentive, when looking for employment, should try to avoid the boss who is a pure Cerebral or a pure Osseous. The Cerebral may be a good planner but his plans and those of the Alimentives will not work well together. The Cerebral can not see the Alimentive's point of view clearly enough to forgive him for his too primitive methods. The pure Osseous boss soon becomes disgusted because the Alimentive is so lacking in system. He usually comes out all right in the end, but the orderly Osseous is too exasperated by what he considers the Alimentive's slackness, to wait for the end.

Localities to Avoid

¶ The Alimentive should avoid all frontiers. He can not work well without conveniences, and since these are few and far between in unsettled regions it is much more difficult for him to be a success there.

Vocations for Pure Alimentives

¶ Cooking, catering, nursing, merchandizing of all food and drink stuffs, the conducting of cafes, restaurants, hotels, cafeterias, rest rooms and all places maintained for the ease, comfort and feeding of mankind, are the general vocations for pure or extreme Alimentives.

Vocations for Alimentive-Thoracics

¶ The merchandizing of the artistic, novel and esthetic in food, clothing and shelter; conducting of tea rooms, confectionery stores, smart specialty and clothing shops. Salesmanship of restricted residence districts, fancy cars, etc.

Vocations for Alimentive-Musculars

¶ The merchandizing of more practical commodities such as potatoes, meat, middle class homes, durable clothing. Alimentive-Muscular women make excellent dressmakers.

Vocations for the Alimentive-Osseous

¶ Merchandizing of farms, ranches, timber, lumber, hardware. Bond salesmanship.

Vocations for Alimentive-Cerebrals

¶ Merchandizing, manufacturing and marketing of food, clothing and shelter commodities on a large scale in world markets. This type combination exists in most of the world's millionaires.

Part Two

VOCATIONS FOR THORACICS

¶ The Thoracic type works best with people. Every person in whom this type predominates will make his greatest success only in vocations bringing him into contact with people.

The Born Entertainer

¶ As we have pointed out, the Thoracic is a born entertainer. His greatest abilities lie in the direction of the stage and all forms of its activities.

Capitalizes His Approbative Instincts

¶ The Thoracic loves the approval and applause of others. He is clever, dazzling, often scintillating, brilliant and magnetic. All these enable him to win fame behind the foot-lights, upon the screen and in many lines of theatrical work. His gregarious instincts also enable him to make a success of work with others.

Chances for Money-Making

¶ His chances for making a great deal of money are excellent. A thousand dollars a week is not an unusual salary for an entertainer and the thousand-dollar-a-night singer is no longer a rarity. These always belong to the Thoracic type, for reasons stated in Chapter II.

Chances for Money-Spending

¶ But when the stage gives him a large income it also furnishes the companions and temptations for spending money freely. Even the Thoracic of fame seldom has much money. Also his own irresponsibility makes it difficult for him to save.

Work to Avoid

¶ The Thoracic should avoid every line of work which has to be done the same way day in and day out. He must avoid routine in every form. Monotonous work is not for him.

Things to Avoid

¶ Things the Thoracic must avoid are the mechanical—for these demand to be used in the same way always. The Thoracic does not like to do anything over and over.

Should Not Work Alone

¶ The Thoracic should never work alone. He should not go into any vocation where he is separated from his fellows. The loneliness and drabness of working away from people are fatal to his best effort.

Business Partners to Select

¶ The Thoracic should select Muscular business partners because of their practicalizing influence. Second choice for him is an Alimentive partner and third is a Thoracic like himself.

Partners and Employees to Avoid

¶ The Thoracic should avoid Osseous employees and Osseous partners, for the reason that this type can no more understand the Thoracic than it can understand the easy-going Alimentive. These two types are at opposite ends of the pole, and to blend them harmoniously in any relationship is almost impossible. The Thoracic employer, who always wants things done instantly, is maddened by the slow, unadaptable Osseous employee.

Bosses to Avoid

¶ For the reasons stated above, every Thoracic person should avoid working for extremely bony people. The Osseous is as much irritated by the rapid-fire reactions of the Thoracic employee as the Thoracic is by the slowness of the Osseous.

Localities to Avoid

¶ The Thoracic individual should avoid all localities which would cut him off from his kind. He should never, except when combined with the Osseous in type, live in remote regions, on the edge of civilization or too far away from neighbors. Companionship is always essential to his happiness and success.

Vocations for the Pure Thoracics

¶ Art, advertising, comic opera, grand opera, concert singing, the stage, the screen and all forms of high class reception work are the lines for pure Thoracics.

For Thoracic-Alimentives

¶ Medicine, merchandizing of artistic, esthetic commodities, life insurance, moving pictures, novelty salesmanship, and demonstrating.

For Thoracic-Musculars

¶ Vocal and instrumental music, interior decoration, politics, social service, advertising, athletics and design.

For Thoracic-Osseous

¶ Landscape gardening, scientific research, the ministry.

For Thoracic-Cerebrals

¶ Authorship, private secretaryship, education, journalism, musical composition, publicity work, photography.

Part Three

VOCATIONS FOR MUSCULARS

¶ The Muscular works best with things. He does not sell them as well as does the Alimentive—for the things he is interested in are not the things that sell but the things that move. He likes to work with high-powered cars, machinery of all kinds, and everything that involves motion. These things, though necessities sometimes and luxuries occasionally, are not such necessities as food, clothing and homes. Therefore there is no such market for them. The automobile has almost made itself a necessity, but even it is not yet as necessary to human happiness as food, clothing or shelter.

The Born Mechanic and Inventor

¶ The Muscular is the born mechanic and inventor. He enjoys working with things he can handle, mold, change, construct and improve with his powerful, efficient hands. Most of the mechanics of the world are Musculars and every inventor has the Muscular element strongly marked in him.

Chances for Money-Making

¶ The Muscular's chances for making money are not as great as those of the Alimentive, for the reason that he deals best with things the world can sometimes get along without. His money-making chances are not as great as those of the Thoracic, for he is not fitted to win the public favor which comes to the latter. Also the Muscular's vocations are not as well paid as those of the two former types, unless his inventions are successful.

The Orator

¶ Oratory furnishes one of the best fields for the Muscular's money-making and fame-achieving opportunities. Every man and woman who has acquired fame or fortune on the public platform has much of the Muscular type in his makeup—always, however, in combination with the Cerebral.

Capitalizes His Activity Instincts

¶ As shown in Chapter III, the Muscular, like the other types, capitalizes his chief instinct. In his case it is the instinct of activity. The Muscular likes activity, so he likes work, and because he is a good worker he nearly always has work to do.

The Muscularly Inclined

¶ Every person Muscularly inclined can make a success at something of a practical nature, in the handling, running, driving, constructing or inventing of machinery.

Things to Avoid

¶ The Muscular should avoid all vocations which confine him within small areas, pin him down to inactivity or sedentary work.

Business Partners to Select
¶ The Musculars should select Musculars as their first choice in business partners, with Cerebrals second and Thoracics third.

Partners and Employees to Avoid
¶ The Muscular should avoid the Osseous partner, the Osseous boss and the Osseous employee because his pugnacity makes it almost impossible for him to work harmoniously with this type.

Localities to Avoid
¶ The Muscular can work in almost any locality. But he should avoid every place which keeps him too closely confined.

Vocations for Pure Musculars
¶ The driving of high-powered cars, airplanes, machinery of all kinds, and work with his hands are the lines in which the average Muscular is most often successful. Other lines for him are construction, civil engineering, mechanics, professional dancing, acrobatics, athletics and pugilism.

Women of this type make splendid physical culture teachers and expert swimmers.

For Muscular-Alimentives
¶ The manufacturing and selling of practical foods, clothing and shelter; also politics.

For Muscular-Thoracics
¶ Advertising, sculpture, osteopathy, athletics, exploration, medicine, baritone and tenor singing, instrumental music, politics, social service, transportation, designing and dentistry.

For Muscular-Osseous
¶ Construction, bridge building, office law, policemen and police women, mechanics, mining.

For Muscular-Cerebrals
¶ Architecture, art, journalism, trial or jury law, oratory, surgery, transportation. Teachers and tragedians also come from this type.

Part Four

VOCATIONS FOR THE OSSEOUS

¶ The Osseous man or woman can do his best work with things. Those with which he works best are lands, forests, the sea, the plains, the mountains and certain kinds of mechanical things.

Instead of combining things and people in his work, like the Alimentive; machines and people, like the Muscular; or people only, like the Thoracic, the Osseous must not only confine himself almost exclusively to working with things, but he must work with them away from the interference or interruption or superintendence of other people.

Capitalizes His Independence Instinct

¶ The Osseous, like other types, succeeds in work which automatically brings into play his basic instincts. His fundamental instinct is that of *independence*. He never succeeds signally in any line of work in which this instinct is repressed or thwarted.

He chafes against restriction, enjoys mastering a thing and when let alone to work in his own way he makes an excellent employee. As has been stated, he is the "steadiest" of all.

Chances for Money-Making

¶ Chances for the Osseous to make a great deal of money are few. Unless he confines himself to finance—working as exclusively with money as possible—or to dealing with natural resources, the Osseous seldom becomes rich.

He cares more for money than any of the other types, saves a much larger portion of what he earns, and no matter how rich, is seldom extravagant. His greatest obstacle to money-making is his tendency to hang on to whatever he has, awaiting the rise in prices which never go quite high enough to suit him.

An Osseous friend of ours has lived for forty years on almost nothing while holding, for a fabulous price, an old residential corner on a desirable block of a downtown street in one of the large American cities. He could have sold it years ago for enough to make him comfortable for life, to give him travel, leisure, comforts and self-expression, but he refused.

As has been pointed out before, each individual prefers the self-expression common to his type. This man has found more of what is real self-expression to him in defying the destruction of this building and the march of commerce in that neighborhood, and in opposing prospective buyers, than all the money-bought comforts in the world could have given him.

So he has worked away as a draughtsman at a small salary eight hours a day for those forty years. He is unmarried and has no brothers or sisters. When he dies remote relatives whom he has never seen and who care nothing for him will sell the property and have a good time on the money.

But they will have no better time spending it than he has had saving it!

Those Who are Inclined to the Osseous

¶ Every person with a large Osseous element is capable of saving money, of being a faithful worker under right conditions and of withstanding hardship in his work. Difficult missions into pioneer regions are successful only when entrusted to men or women who have the Osseous as one of their first two elements.

The North Pole

¶ It is a significant fact that all the men who have made signal efforts at finding the North and South Poles have possessed the bony as a large proportion of their makeup. No extremely fat man has ever attempted such a thing.

Missionaries

¶ It is also interesting to note that the most successful missionaries have had a larger-than-average bony system and that all those who go into the extreme edges of civilization and stay there any length of time are largely of this type.

Other types plan to become missionaries and some get as far as to be sent somewhere, but those who stick, who spend years in the far corners of the earth, are always largely Osseous.

Things to Avoid

¶ The Osseous must avoid all vocations demanding his constant or intimate contact with large numbers of people, every kind of work that calls for instantaneous movements, sudden adaptations to environment, many or sudden decisions, or crowded workrooms. *He must avoid working for, with, under or over others.*

Business Partners to Select

¶ The Osseous should never have a partner if he can help it.

When he can not help it, he should choose a person of large Cerebral tendencies, for no other type will stand for his peculiarities.

Partners and Employees to Avoid

¶ He should avoid, above all things, a partner who is Osseous like himself. An Osseous always knows what he wants to do, how he wants to do it, and when. And one of the requirements with him usually is that it must be the opposite of the thing, manner and time desired by the other fellow.

So in business, as in marriage, two Osseous people find themselves in unending warfare. He should avoid the Osseous employee also for the same reasons, and choose the only types that will submit to his hard driving.

Bosses to Avoid

¶ The Osseous should never work for a boss when he has brains enough to work alone. He is so independent that it is almost impossible for him to take orders, and the "contrary streak" in him runs so deep that he is just naturally against what others want him to do.

He is the most insubordinate of all types as an employee and as a boss is the most inexorable.

Localities to Avoid

¶ The Osseous should avoid all congested communities. He does not belong in the city. Except in some vocation where he handles money, he seldom succeeds in a metropolis.

His field is the frontier—the great open spaces of land, sea, forest and mountain—where he works with things that grow, that are not sensitive, that do not offer human resistance to his imperious, dominating nature.

Vocations for Pure Osseous

¶ Farming, stock-raising, lumbering, lighthouse keeping, open-sea fishing, hardware, saw-milling and all pioneering activities are the vocations in which the unmixed Osseous succeeds best.

For Osseous-Alimentives

¶ Work as a farm hand, sheep or cattle herder, or truck gardener are the lines in which this combination succeeds best. He can do clerical work also.

For Osseous-Thoracics

¶ Agriculture, carpentering, railroading, mining, office law, electrical and chemical engineering are the first choices for this combination. Both men and women of this type succeed on police forces also.

For Osseous-Cerebrals

¶ The invention of intricate mechanical devices is something in which this combination often succeeds. Other lines for him are those of statistician, mathematician, proof-reader, expert accountant, genealogist and banker.

Part Five

VOCATIONS FOR CEREBRALS

¶ The Cerebral man or woman can never be happy or successful until he is in work that deals with ideas. But his planning is often impractical and for this reason he does not succeed when working independently as does the Osseous.

Capitalizes His Cerebrative Instinct

¶ The Cerebral gets his name from the cerebrum or thinking part of the brain, because this is the system most highly evolved in him. Its great size in the large-headed man causes it to dominate his life.

Thus his chief instinct is cerebration—dreaming, meditating, visualizing, planning. Since these are the real starters of all progress this type should be encouraged, with a view to making him more practical.

The Born Writer

¶ The brain system is large in all men and women who achieve distinction in writing, or in other lines where the brain does most of the work. Unless combined with the Muscular, this man writes much better than he talks and usually avoids speech-making. When the Muscular is combined with the Cerebral he will be an excellent lecturer or teacher.

Chances for Money-Making

¶ The pure Cerebral has the least likelihood of making money of any of the types, for the reasons stated in Chapter V.

If he is a pure Cerebral his ideas and writings, however brilliant, will seldom bring him financial independence unless he gets a Muscular, Thoracic or Alimentive business manager and strictly follows his directions.

The Cerebrally Inclined

¶ Any person inclined to the Cerebral type—that is, with a large, wide, high forehead or a large head for his body—will succeed in some line of work where study and mental effort are required.

Things to Avoid

¶ The pure Cerebral should avoid every kind of work that calls for manual or bodily effort, physical strenuosity, lifting of heavy things, or the handling of large machines. He should avoid every kind of work that gives no outlet for planning or thinking. He should avoid being an employer because he sees the employee's viewpoint so clearly that he lives in his skin instead of his own. This means that he does not get the service out of employees that other types get.

He is not fitted in any way to rule others, dislikes to dominate them, feels like apologizing all the time for compelling them to do things, and is made generally miserable by this responsibility.

Business Partners to Select

¶ The selection of a partner is one of greater importance to the Cerebral than to any other type, for it is almost impossible for him to work out his plans alone.

It is as necessary for the Cerebral to have a partner as it is for the Osseous not to have one.

This partner should be a person largely of the Muscular type, to supply the practicality the Cerebral lacks. As a second choice he should be of the Thoracic type, to supply the gregariousness which the Cerebral lacks. The third choice should be an Osseous, to supply the quality which can get work out of employees and thus make up for the lax treatment the Cerebral tends to give his subordinates.

Partners and Employees to Avoid

¶ Though he succeeds well when he is himself a combination of Alimentive and Cerebral, the pure Cerebral should avoid partners and employees who are purely Alimentive. Their ideas and attitudes are too far away from his own for them to succeed co-operatively.

Localities to Avoid

¶ The Cerebral can work in any locality, partly from the fact that every spot in the world interests him. But he should avoid ranches, livestock farms, lumber camps, construction gangs, ditch-digging and saw-milling jobs, for he lacks the physical strength to stand up to them.

Vocations for Pure Cerebrals

¶ Education, teaching, library work, authorship, literary criticism, and philosophy are the vocations best fitted to the pure Cerebral.

For Cerebral-Alimentives

¶ This combination comprises the majority of the world's millionaires, for it combines the intense alimentive desires for life's comforts with the extreme brain capacity necessary to get them. So he becomes a "magnate," a man of "big business," and tends to high finance, manufacturing and merchandizing on a world-scale.

For Cerebral-Thoracics

¶ Journalism, the ministry, teaching, photography, interior decorating, magazine editing, are among the vocations best suited to this type. The best educational directors for large department stores and other establishments, and some of the best comedians, belong to this combination.

For Cerebral-Musculars

¶ Manual education, trial or jury law, invention of all kinds of machinery, social service, oratory, teaching, lecturing, and nose and throat surgery are the best lines of work for this combination.

For Cerebral-Osseous

¶ Authorship, finance, statistics, invention of complex mechanical devices, expert accounting and mathematics are the best lines for this combination.

¶ SO HERE, THEN, ENDETH "*THE FIVE HUMAN TYPES*," BEING THE FIRST VOLUME IN THE WORLD TO EXPOUND SCIENCE'S DISCOVERY THAT ALL HUMAN BEINGS FALL INTO FIVE DEFINITE DIVISIONS ACCORDING TO THEIR BIOLOGICAL EVOLUTION. BY *ELSIE LINCOLN BENEDICT*, FIRST WRITER AND PUBLISHER OF THIS CLASSIFICATION, FIRST LECTURER IN THE WORLD TO PRESENT IT TO THE PUBLIC, AND FIRST COMPILER OF THE SCIENCE OF *HUMAN ANALYSIS*. ALSO BY *RALPH PAINE BENEDICT*, WHOSE KNOWLEDGE AND CO-OPERATION INSPIRED THE DOING OF ALL THESE, PRINTED AND MADE INTO A BOOK BY THE ROYCROFTERS AT THEIR SHOPS WHICH ARE AT EAST AURORA, ERIE COUNTY AND STATE OF NEW YORK, IN THE YEAR NINETEEN HUNDRED AND TWENTY-ONE.

www.ingramcontent.com/pod-product-compliance
Lightning Source LLC
Chambersburg PA
CBHW070654290526
45790CB00001B/313